KT-592-097

Inclusive Play

Practical Strategies for Working with Children aged 3 to 8

Theresa Casey

P·C·P

Paul Chapman
Publishing

CLASS	BARCODE
372.21	R87688
DATE 3 0 JUN 2006	
SOUTH KENT COLLEGE ASHFORD LEARNING CENTRE	

© Theresa Casey 2005

First published 2005
Reprinted 2006

Apart from any fair dealing for the purposes of research or private study, or criticism or review, as permitted under the Copyright, Designs and Patents Act, 1988, this publication may be reproduced, stored or transmitted in any form, or by any means, only with the prior permission in writing of the publishers, or in the case of reprographic reproduction, in accordance with the terms of licences issued by the Copyright Licensing Agency. Enquiries concerning reproduction outside those terms should be sent to the publishers.

Paul Chapman Publishing
A SAGE Publications Company
1 Oliver's Yard
55 City Road
London EC1Y 1SP

SAGE Publications Inc
2455 Teller Road
Thousand Oaks, California 91320

SAGE Publications India Pvt Ltd
B-42, Panchsheel Enclave
Post Box 4109
New Delhi 110 017

Library of Congress Control Number: 2005921840

A catalogue record for this book is available from the British Library

ISBN-10 1-4129-0242-8   ISBN-13 978-1-4129-0242-7
ISBN-10 1-4129-0243-6 (pbk)   ISBN-13 978-1-4129-0243-4 (pbk)

Typeset by Pantek Arts Ltd, Maidstone, Kent
Printed in Great Britain by the Cromwell Press, Trowbridge, Wilts

Dedicated to the memory of my Dad, John James Casey, and
with love for my radiant girl Niamh

Contents

Acknowledgements   *viii*

Introduction   *1*

1   Inclusive play in the early years   4

2   The value of inclusive play   18

3   Creating and sustaining inclusive play environments   31

4   Enabling inclusive play environments – the role of adults   56

5   Inclusive play: creative input   69

6   Working together   86

7   Managing for inclusive play   97

Useful information   *108*

Bibliography   *123*

Index   *126*

Acknowledgements

The Play Inclusive (P.inc) Action Research project led by Susan Macintyre at The Yard adventure playground in Edinburgh grounded this book in real experiences and provided the sparks to set off new questions and ideas.

Thanks for inspiration and fun to the team of staff, volunteers and families past and present of The Yard (Scotland Yard Adventure Centre) and especially our original team of Alison Harper, Mike Worobec, Betty Ferrier and Alan Rees.

Thanks for wise words from:
Margaret Westwood
Fiona Clark and Graeme Nicol of Edinburgh Inclusive
Shirley Thomson and Louise Woodward of the Play Action Team
Sandy Howe and Joyce Gilbert of the Royal School of Dunkeld.

Thank you to the staff and children for kindly allowing me take photographs at:
Balgreen Nursery School, Edinburgh
Millbank Primary School, Nairn
St John's RC Primary School, Edinburgh
The Royal School of Dunkeld
The Yard, Edinburgh
and Penny Martin at Grounds for Learning for putting me in touch.

Thanks for support, encouragement and minding the baby to Tricia, Jessica, Caroline, Veronica and Barbara Casey, Jake, Molly and Eoghan, and as ever and always Jimmy Hewitt.

Introduction

Somewhere in play is a conundrum. Play can be deeply serious or as light as air. It can be loud, abrasive, rude, smutty, hilarious, gentle or tender. It can fully absorb the whole attention of a child or of a group of children and yet can also be frivolous, throw-away or fleeting. It can be dangerous, dark and alarming. It can look like play and not be play, or vice versa.

We recognize the joyousness, the delight of play. We know the sound of children at play and we recognize the expression of play. It can captivate us.

When we reflect seriously on play, examining it closely, we see its amazing complexity. And yet it is really very simple too. It is fun, natural, social; children know how to play without being taught. It is complex and simple at the same time.

Inclusive play embraces dimensions of richness, diversity, appreciation of difference and is both simple and complex too. By aiming for inclusive play we are simply aiming for the best play experiences we can offer to all children. We want play opportunities to be full of possibilities with which the children can engage and questions that they can pose for themselves. It recognizes that children, including children with disabilities or additional support needs, are active seekers and makers of meaning. They are explorers, discoverers and experimenters.

Through play they are making sense of the world around them: people, identities, concepts, elements, dreams, reality, unreality. The practice of providing for play and inclusive play is the same, but aiming for 'inclusion' demands a continual awareness of, and engagement with, the needs and aspirations of the children. It is simple and complex, engaging, easy and demanding at the same time.

There is an increasing emphasis on 'inclusion' in children's settings as in wider society. A broad definition of 'inclusion' relates not only to children with disabilities or additional support needs being included but also to ensuring that all children feel valued and welcomed. And so we increasingly ask ourselves what we can do to achieve the ideals of inclusion in our own settings.

There are many ways that play can be interpreted or defined (there is no definitive answer to questions such as 'what is play?' and 'what is it for?') but in children's settings we do recognize that opportunities for play, along with opportunities for sustained talk and first-hand experiences, are the primary mode for children to actively engage in their own construction of knowledge and meaning.

Play brings a raft of benefits in all areas of the children's being, well-being and development. Time spent playing is the natural arena for forming friendships, finding soul-mates and negotiating relationships. As well as these crucial social experiences, time spent at play is significant to how children view their whole experience of the settings they spend time in and for children with disabilities, to their whole experience of inclusion.

Inclusive Play: Practical Strategies for Working with Children aged 3 to 8 comes about through experience of developing and enabling inclusive play in a number of settings and therefore identifying the contribution it has to make. This book draws on contemporary research, in particular the findings of the Play Inclusive (P.inc) Action Research project. This was a two-year project looking at the ways in which play supports inclusion of children with disabilities, funded in 2002–04 by the Scottish Executive.

The book links recent research with practice, with the aim of providing practitioners with the required understanding and confidence to facilitate inclusive play, and examples that can be applied to a range of settings for three- to eight-year-olds.

Inclusive play is put into the context of children's needs, the current state of knowledge about the benefits of play and also the current policy and guidance context in the UK.

Aiming for inclusive play is crucial across the range of settings that children encounter in their early years. We may sometimes experience difficulty in marrying the desire to provide for truly free and spontaneous play opportunities as a process within the constraints of our settings or professions. Sometimes pressure to achieve set goals can divert our attention away from how we achieve them, from the processes that children go through in creating for themselves meaningful, enriching and sustaining experiences.

The book addresses inclusive play in a way that allows practitioners to apply the ideas and strategies flexibly in their own settings – nurseries, out-of-school provision, schools or playschemes. The approach encourages us as practitioners to actively consider the particular needs of our whole setting in order to tailor our approach appropriately.

The benefits of inclusive play contribute to the life of the setting as a whole and the creation of a positive ethos from which everyone will benefit. Equally, inclusion is a responsibility shared by everyone in a setting, encompassing our own interactions as teams and communities, as well as those between the children.

Different cultures (historical, local, professional, team and organizational among them) may be at work within different settings and professions. These can significantly colour the extent to which individuals feel able to participate in the processes of developing inclusive play. Practitioners often feel pressure from the conflicting demands such as curriculum goals, professional expectations and inspections. A continuity of approach is proposed, based on a view of children as active learners and on play as their mode of gathering and using authentic experiences. You are asked to consider how this can be applied in different settings and how inclusive play relates to different professional roles. Implicit in this, for some of us, will be a challenge to step beyond some professional boundaries and perhaps gather up some courage to step out of a personal comfort zone, working in partnership with children and other practitioners.

Terminology

Children

There are different views of the use of terms such as 'children with disabilities', 'disabled children' and 'children with additional support needs'. The phrase 'disabled children' is now preferred in some contexts. It reflects the concept that the child is disabled by barriers in society rather than by a particular impairment. There are many children and parents who do not like it, however, since it seems to emphasize 'disabled' over the child. The phrase 'children with additional support needs' reflects a broader sense of a requirement to respond to children's varied needs which may change over time. The phrase can encompass a broad spectrum: children who are experiencing difficulties or change, gifted children, refugees and asylum-seeking children, for example.

This book is about ways of ensuring that children are included in play and, through play, included in their setting. Therefore, in most cases I have not found it necessary to describe children in terms of a particular impairment, need or circumstance. The reader should assume that when we talk about children we are talking about children with a range of abilities, personalities, needs, backgrounds, talents and interests – and that these can change from day to day, if not minute to minute!

Short descriptions and case studies of children at play in the book are 'composite' pictures drawn from different settings and experiences. They are intended to illustrate types of experience, interventions and processes. Names and details therefore do not identify any particular child or place.

Parents

Throughout this book I have chosen to use the words 'parent' or 'parents' to mean the people who care for the child: mothers, fathers, foster carers or temporary care-givers, step-parents, grandparents, single parents, heterosexual or same sex couples.

Teams

This book is for people working with children in a wide variety of settings. I have generally used the terms 'practitioners' or 'teams' to include people in the setting who can contribute to the experience of inclusive play. Inclusive play is more likely to take place within settings where inclusion is part of the ethos. Therefore teams might include teachers, playworkers, specialist staff, volunteers, senior staff, janitors, nursery nurses, learning support staff, bus escorts, parents, visiting staff – the people who make up the community of the setting.

Inclusive play in the early years

This chapter provides an introduction to key concepts which underpin inclusive play.

- ■ What is inclusive play?

- ■ Why should we include children? A look at children's rights and the law, values and principles.

- ■ Factors influencing inclusive play in early years settings – opportunities, barriers and challenges.

- ■ Relating inclusive play to the values and curricula of early years settings in the UK.

What is 'inclusive play'?

The word 'inclusive' has now entered our thinking and pops up in relation to schools, recreation, communities and education. It reflects an aspiration to ensure that everyone can take part, be included, can participate. Inclusion can mean very different things to different people in different settings and is perhaps in danger of being one of those words that come and go and lose any real meaning. It demands that we ask ourselves questions. What do we really mean when we use the word 'inclusive'? What does it suggest about our practice and goals, or the philosophy of the setting? Does it reflect the experience of the children who use the service or setting? Is it there simply to tick a box?

By coupling the word 'inclusive' with the word 'play' we really have created a phrase open to interpretation! Play has been examined from the points of view of many disciplines – anthropology, sociology, pedagogy, psychology and human geographies, among them. They ask questions such as: How do we recognize play? What is it for? How do children benefit from play? Is play for children the same as play among animals or adults? A definition of play has long been elusive.

A neat summing up came in a recent review of play, which took play to mean 'what children and young people do when they follow their own ideas, in their own way and for their own reasons' (DCMS, 2004: 9).

Another useful definition and description of play that emphasizes the child's owner-ship of his or her play, and is widely accepted in the field of playwork, is that 'play is freely chosen, personally directed, intrinsically motivated behaviour that actively engages the child' (NPFA, 2000: 6).

Play is often described as having a quality of otherness about it: that in play we become detached from the 'real' world and can enter a world of imagination, transformation and creativity. We can be carried away, embark on whimsy and flights of fancy. There are no concrete rules or fixed expectations. We can be completely absorbed in play until the world around as interrupts or the impulse fades.

For all that it is very difficult to pin down, the importance of play to children is well recognized and is considered fundamental among practitioners working with young children. To illustrate this, the following quotes regard children's play in the Foundation Stage for three- to five-year-olds in England, in the new Foundation Phase for three- to seven-year-olds in Wales, and in Pre-School Settings in Northern Ireland.

> Well-planned play, both indoors and outdoors, is a key way in which young children learn with enjoyment and challenge. In playing, they behave in dif-ferent ways: sometimes their play will be boisterous, sometimes they will describe and discuss what they are doing, sometimes they will be quiet and reflective as they play.
>
> (QCA, 2000: 25)

> Children learn through first hand experiential activities with the serious business of 'play' providing the vehicle. Through their play, children prac-tise and consolidate their learning, play with ideas, experiment, take risks, solve problems, and make decisions individually, in small and in large groups. First hand experiences allow children to develop an understanding of themselves and the world in which they live. The development of chil-dren's self-image and feelings of self-worth and self-esteem are at the core of this phase.
>
> (Qualifications, Curriculum and Assessment Authority for Wales, 2004: 2)

> Young children require opportunities to investigate, satisfy their curiosity, explore the environment inside and outside the playroom, extend their sense of wonder, experience success and develop a positive attitude towards learning; young children require appropriate periods of time for learning through sustained involvement in play.
>
> (NICCEA, 1997: 7)

Children gain first hand experience of the world through play.

Since play is so important to children and to us as practitioners, empathy, experience and a simple sense of fairness tell us that including children in, and through, play is an aspiration worth working towards. Therefore time spent considering what these terms mean to us is time very well spent.

The following short exercises can be used to explore what play and inclusion mean in our settings. They should involve as many different people as possible from the community of the setting and can be adapted to use with children as a way of exploring their experience of inclusion and play (suggestions are given below).

What do we mean by inclusion?

'Inclusion' is now a commonly used term but the meaning may be neither clear nor shared. This activity aims to spark discussion and reflection.

- Copy the page of 'Inclusion discussion starters' (opposite) and cut into separate slips.

- Lay these face down. A member of the group should pick one at random and read it out.

- This person kicks off the discussion by sharing any thoughts or questions it brings to mind.

- Other members of the group should be encouraged to join in the discussion.

- Use as many or as few of the discussion starters as seems appropriate.

- One member of the group can be designated as the reader if that is more appropriate to the group.

Further discussion points

- Does the discussion suggest a common understanding or definition of 'inclusion' within the group?

- How does this compare with the practice in your setting?

Inclusion discussion starters

- Inclusion means being social, being part of the group, being together.

- For inclusion to work, children should get one-to-one support to prepare and support them into mainstream. They do need lots of help and preparation first.

- Inclusion means being allowed to be who you want to be.

- I just want to be with who I want to be with, hanging out really.

- I know that inclusion will probably never happen as everything gravitates towards what's normal and what's acceptable and what we can all relate to. People like to pigeon-hole other people and if they are different they think 'oh, they don't fit in'.

- The more successful schools are in achieving inclusive outcomes for their pupils, the better are the chances that these young people will go on and prosper in later life and achieve broader social inclusion in society. (HM Inspectorate of Education, *Count Us In: Achieving Inclusion in Scottish Schools*, 2002: 3)

- You are on a committee planning a conference which aims to highlight the 'importance of inclusive play'. What would you put on the agenda and why?

- Inclusion means a deep commitment and awareness that there is a very wide range of human behaviour and understanding of the world; that there is a respect for different perceptions of life.

- In a school setting inclusion can mean that the total environment has meaning and is accessible to everybody: that it is safe; that it is clear what everything is for; that it is functional.

- If the children are all just absorbed in their own thing, I don't think that is inclusion.

Further discussion starters specific to your setting can easily be created by:

- looking for definitions of inclusion in policy and guidelines documents, in statements from disability, play or children's rights organizations, or on the Internet;

- asking children, parents and colleagues for their definitions. Try using a dictaphone to quickly capture some views. This is a nice way to adapt the activity for children;

- gathering visual discussion starters such as photographs, pictures from newspapers or video clips.

© Theresa Casey, *Inclusive Play*, Paul Chapman Publishing, 2005.

Memories of play

- Each person is given a piece of good quality paper and a choice of drawing materials such as charcoal, soft pencils or watercolours. Offering good quality materials helps to bring a sense of value to the process.

- Spend around ten minutes thinking about a favourite memory of play from your childhood. It may be about a particular place, person or type of experience and about the time of year, how you felt, who was there.

- Use the materials to draw, write or suggest an impression of this memory.

- Bring the group back together and in turn share these memories.

- Sum up some of the main themes that emerge. These are often:

  - a sense of freedom and excitement;

  - elements of danger and risk;

  - playing in, and with, the natural environment;

  - breaking taboos and seeking out forbidden places;

  - freedom from adult involvement.

Further discussion points

- What does it suggest if we compare these themes to children's play opportunities nowadays or in our own settings?

- Are the changes that have taken place or new restrictions placed on children's play reasonable and for the good of the children? Where do they come from?

- Do all children need and benefit from these types of experiences?

(This exercise may be familiar to people working in play, but it is always useful as a reminder of the importance of play. It is also a very enjoyable way of getting to know colleagues better and to open up discussion.)

Follow-on activities

The activities below will help to raise awareness of play and can be used to motivate teams to consider inclusive play more fully.

- Obtain a copy of the United Nations *Convention on the Rights of the Child* and look for rights relevant to play and inclusion (see Useful information).

- Ask your team to collect articles and stories related to play and inclusion from newspapers and magazines, over about a week or so. Bring these back together and consider questions such as:

  - How are children with additional support needs represented?

  - What are the common attitudes to children?

  - What is suggested about how play and play settings are viewed?

  - Are children's own views and opinions reported?

- Dedicate some shelf space to inclusive play in your staffroom or office, to which everyone can contribute resources.

The case for inclusive play: why should we try to include all children?

Children's rights

The United Nations Convention on the Rights of the Child (UNCRC) articulates the rights of children and the standards to which all governments must aspire in realizing these rights for all children. The Convention is the most universally accepted human rights instrument in history and was ratified by the UK government in 1991. By doing so the government has committed to protecting and ensuring children's rights and has agreed to be held accountable for this commitment before the international community.

There are four key articles in the Convention which relate directly to inclusive play – Articles 1, 2, 23 and 31.

- **Articles 1 and 2** ensure that the rights expressed in the convention apply to every child under the age of 18 without 'discrimination of any kind'.

- **Article 23** recognizes that disabled children should 'enjoy a full and decent life, in conditions that ensure dignity, promote self-reliance and facilitate the child's active participation in the community'.

- Through **Article 31**, children have the right to play. It 'recognizes the right of the child to rest and leisure, and to engage in play and recreational activities appropriate to the age of the child and to participate freely in cultural life and the arts' (UNICEF, 1989).

Between them, these rights make a powerful case for ensuring that all children are welcomed into our settings and that their right to be there is not only respected but actively promoted.

It's the law!

■ The Disability Discrimination Act 1995 (DDA) brought in laws to end discrimination against disabled people (including children) and is applicable to England, Wales and Scotland.

■ It is unlawful to refuse a service or offer a lower standard of service to disabled people, and as of 2004 service providers are required to make changes to the physical environment where aspects of it make it impossible for disabled people to access a service. There are requirements to make reasonable adjustments to policies, practices and procedures that discriminate against disabled people.

■ The DDA is 'anticipatory', which means that children's services will need to show that they are planning and acting to remove barriers and to develop inclusive settings and services.

■ The Special Educational Needs and Disability Act 2001 (SENDA) brought in duties in relation to education which were not covered by the DDA, and outlaws any form of discrimination against disabled pupils currently attending school, or against prospective pupils.

■ The Disability Rights Commission (DRC) was set up in April 2000 to oversee the legislation. It has powers of enforcement and issues codes of practice in relation to the DDA (see Useful information).

■ The Children Act 1989 states principles in relation to disabled children, including that a primary aim should be to promote access for all children to the same range of services and that the views of children and parents should be sought and taken into account.

■ Legislation is available from The Stationery Office (see Useful information) and can be downloaded from www.hmso.gov.uk.

Values and principles

Medical and social models of disability

The medical and social medical models of disability reflect two ways in which disability is understood. They influence how people react to, think about and act towards disabled children and adults.

The medical model views disabled children as having an illness or problem that needs to be cured. This illness or problem is a hurdle which they need to get over in order to take part in 'normal' society. They require help from experts who are in the best position to determine what will be the most suitable treatment for them. If they cannot be cured then they should be cared for. This attitude is very pervasive in many societies and lots of us have unconsciously absorbed aspects of it.

The social model of disability was developed by disabled people as a challenge to the medical model. The social model recognizes that some people are disabled by barriers in society that exclude and discriminate against them, for example through attitudes that favour non-disabled children and adults, through physical barriers and in the way we organize things. Let's have a look at a few examples of each of these from children's settings.

- The assumption that all disabled children will require one-to-one assistance thereby allowing children to be excluded on the basis of not being able to afford enough staff.

- Having equipment stored in cupboards with written labels only, with the consequence that some children are stopped from making independent choices because they do not know what equipment is stored where.

- Entrance criteria which insist that only children from the local school can attend the provision thereby excluding children who attend special schools or units.

Removing these attitudinal, environmental and organizational barriers is a priority within the social model. It is also the approach taken in this book.

Integration or inclusion?

The terms 'integration' and 'inclusion' are sometimes used interchangeably and often very loosely. Integration tends to suggest that disabled children can be part of a children's setting if they are able to adapt to it. This places the emphasis on ensuring the child is equipped with particular skills or has achieved particular standards so that he or she is able to fit in.

Inclusion has a broader meaning, placing the onus on our settings to ensure that we are open and prepared to welcome children with a range of abilities, backgrounds and personalities as a matter of course; that we respect the right of the child to be there and expect to provide a high quality experience for all.

The move from a concept of 'integration' towards 'inclusion' reflects a progression in the thinking about the rights of disabled children in society and about the roles of settings and institutions such as schools.

If we accept that play is fundamental to children and their experience of childhood (and the fact that it is expressed as a right in Article 31 of the UNCRC suggests that we do) then aiming for inclusion naturally follows. It can be argued that provision which is not inclusive cannot truly be of good quality either. The lessons children learn are that only youngsters like themselves are welcome, that adults value them but not others, and that there is a narrow range of behaviour and people that are acceptably 'normal'.

Factors influencing inclusive play in early years settings – opportunities, barriers and challenges

Opportunities

- Play provides an important arena for forming, negotiating and maintaining friendships and relationships and is therefore particularly important for children's sense of belonging.

- Play is formally recognized as crucial to early years practice, which gives practitioners permission and the responsibility to really focus on developing play in their settings.

- The nature of play is that there are no 'right ways' and 'wrong ways' of playing; therefore, differences in being and doing can easily be accommodated, welcomed and celebrated in the setting.

- Welcoming and celebrating richness and diversity creates an atmosphere of trust and acceptance which allows all the children to feel that who they are is important and valued.

- Play environments develop, change and evolve according to the changing needs and interests of the children. The creativity of early years practitioners will support this process. (See Chapter 3 for more details on developing the play environment.)

- Early years practitioners are important people. You are an early role model outside the home. You are in an ideal position to challenge, support and widen children's experience of the world.

- Teams in early years settings are able to model inclusive behaviour, practice and attitudes in the way we work with each other and the children. (See Chapter 4 for more details.)

- By its nature, providing for play means responding to children as they are at that moment, without imposing adult agendas or goals.

Barriers

- The most basic and pervasive barriers to developing more inclusive settings are attitudes, assumptions and stereotypes.

- We unconsciously 'learn' attitudes that reflect the medical model – that disabled children need to be cared for, that experts are required, that special provision is more appropriate.

- Assumptions about inclusion also act as barriers. Common ones are that all disabled children automatically require one-to-one support and that the setting will have to buy special equipment.

■ Stereotypes about disability abound – for example, that all children with Down's syndrome are warm and affectionate or that children with autistic spectrum disorders are shut off in their own worlds. Stereotypes such as these have serious repercussions as they can be the basis of decisions such as whether or not a child is given a place in a setting. They fail to recognize the child as an individual and instead fit him or her into a perceived group.

■ Fears relate to assumptions and stereotypes of this sort, for example fear that the other children will be adversely affected by too much staff time being taken up with children in need of extra support; fear that staff won't be able to cope with unfamiliar or challenging behaviour, different communication methods or with specific needs such as epilepsy.

■ Physical barriers include physical access to settings and equipment but also to the sensory environment (for example, unsuitable lighting, poor acoustics).

■ Organizational barriers range from more visible ones, such as entrance criteria, to less visible ones, such as inflexible adherence to timetabling that causes a child difficultly in coping.

■ Although curricula across the UK are now emphasizing play, there are still conflicting imperatives that squeeze play out from the day.

Challenges – finding ways to make it work

■ Barriers tend to grow – they are like unpruned hedges! Leaving stereotypes, attitudes and assumptions unchallenged allows them to take root and flourish.

■ Many of us, in the usual course of things, have never got to know a disabled child well. Because of the way that provision is organized, if we have worked with children with disabilities it may well have been in a special setting for children with one type of impairment. Because we have not encountered inclusive play working well it can be hard to picture it.

■ Resistance to change can be overwhelming at times. Change can be exciting but can also be scary. Accepting the need to do things differently isn't always easy.

■ Early years settings are a good start for inclusive play. Making it work there means that children and their families are building up experience and confidence that it can work elsewhere. They will be happier to go on to other inclusive opportunities knowing that they can explain what support the child really requires, what works and what doesn't.

■ Finding ways to demystify inclusive play by allowing people to experience inclusive play and settings and to get a feel for it can really help. Ideally this can be done by visiting inclusive play settings, through experiential learning or by using resources that show it working. It can also be achieved through:

- training – in disability equality and awareness, playwork, and in particular techniques, methods or approaches that will help us to respond to the actual needs of children;

- information-gathering via the Internet, from specific organizations, from other practitioners and from talking things through with the child and his or her family;

- establishing systems of support from experienced practitioners who can make practical suggestions and help to unpick some of the stereotypes.

Inclusive play and the curricula of early years settings

There are very interesting divergences and developments taking place across the UK as new curricula are piloted and evolved. Recognition of the role of play is coming to the fore, while many settings are properly getting down to the business of grappling with inclusion to make it work.

The current placing of play and inclusion is identified to a lesser or greater degree within the plethora of 'stages' and 'phases' in the curricula across the UK, in the development of play policies, and in the growth of national organizations for play such as the Children's Play Council, Play Wales, Play Scotland and PlayBoard (see Useful information). It would be logical to expect that inclusive play should be an outcome of these strands, though it is by no means inevitable.

Despite the recognition of play, changes to curricula and therefore practice take time and energy and some practitioners may feel pressure from one direction to maintain the status quo while being urged, from another direction, to embrace change.

Some practitioners are in the position where their sole or most important goal is to provide for play (such as adventure playground workers) while other practitioners will perhaps see play as a 'vehicle' for learning, health or social goals. Yet adventure playground workers will still want to ask themselves why they provide for play in the way that they do and whether what they offer is as wide and as enriching as it could be. Likewise, early years practitioners in an education setting, for example, might also want to ask themselves whether, while acting within curricular guidance, they have managed to offer the children authentic and meaningful experiences.

We mentioned earlier that play can be described as a mode or a mindset. It is a way of doing things or even approaching doing things (or nothing!) rather than a set of activities or tasks. Set in relation to curricular goals, stepping stones or targets, we sometimes find it difficult to marry the two. As Adams et al. (2004: 11) commented: 'there are more ways than one of reaching a specified goal or outcome ... Specifying a large number of end points to a process, however highly valued they may be, can never guarantee the quality of the process itself.' Aiming for inclusive play is about process and makes a contribution to the range and quality of experiences children gain from the settings in which they spend their time.

In this chapter we have started to look at what inclusive play means in early years settings and have touched on the idea that providing for inclusive play is the same, if perhaps an extension, as doing our best in providing for play. Before leaving this idea and moving on to the benefits of play it will be useful to look again at what we provide and how it squares up to frameworks for play provision. There are a number of quality assessment frameworks for play available (see Useful information), but as a starting point the 'Best Play' objectives are extremely useful.

> The objectives are broad statements, which are intended to set out how the definition of play and the underpinning values and principles should be put into practice.
>
> (NPFA, 2000: 18)

The 'Best Play' objectives (see Figure 1.1) prompt us to think about our practice and the opportunities we aim to provide and to ask questions such as 'how do we meet this objective, to what extent and for which children?'

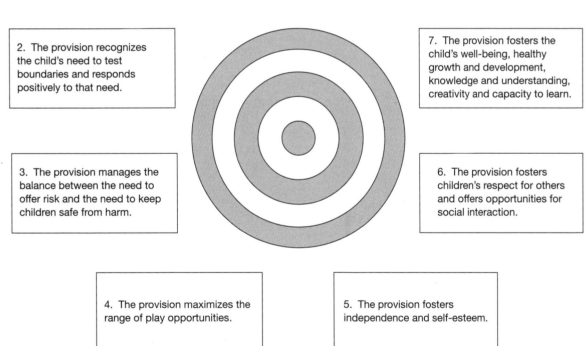

Fig. 1.1 Using the 'Best Play' objectives (NPFA, 2000: 18) as an evaluation tool.

© Theresa Casey, *Inclusive Play*, Paul Chapman Publishing, 2005.

Figure 1.1 suggests one way in which the objectives can be adapted for use as an evaluation tool. Working in small groups, consider to what extent the play opportunities in your setting meet each of the objectives. Draw an arrow from each objective to the target to represent this.

- Hitting the centre of the target = really getting this right.

- Further away = meet this objective partially or some of the time.

- Outside ring = rarely meet this objective.

- Or, missed the target altogether!

You might like to adapt this by thinking about a particular child and asking how and to what extent the provision meets the objective for him or her. Detailed notes of the evidence for this would be useful documentation to inform planning and practice.

Young children can be included in using this framework to participate in evaluation themselves, for example by:

- adapting the language of each objective to make it meaningful to them;

- using visual references;

- allowing the children to work in small groups with adult support as necessary;

- considering one objective at a time.

CASE STUDY

The school hall is being transformed into a sparkly winter wonderland. Floor to ceiling is becoming crisp and frosty, icicles made of cellophane and glitter hang from the ceiling, icy chandeliers made from willow and tinsel spin and reflect the light. Twinkling fairly lights catch the eye in a corner and a blue cave made from boxes and papier mâché is enticing the children.

We have been working all day on this transformation, staff and children together. But now it is almost done, everyone is tired and relaxed and there is a low hum of chat and laughter. Some staff and children are still making lovely additions to the scene. One of the adults is so engrossed she has really forgotten about the children and is completely engaged in sticking shiny stars to a deep velvet backdrop. Junk materials and sparkly, crinkly bits and pieces are scattered all over the floor (although someone is carefully keeping a corner free of clutter and noise, making a quiet retreat). Lots of the children are having fun playing with the leftovers – there is a wee group prancing around decorated with garlands and ribbons.

Jess is sitting in her wheelchair in among the hubbub, enjoying the atmosphere and the visual stimulation provided by the movement, colour and light. A member of staff is sitting near her quietly making paper chains and looking up and chatting with her from time to time. Other children talk to them both as they pass or stop and share what they are doing for a moment.

Neil is sitting right in the middle of the floor surrounded by sparkling paper and fabrics, tossing them in the air and laughing, or pulling them towards his face to feel them.

SUMMARY

■ It is important to spend time as teams exploring what we mean by inclusive play and how that relates to the practice in our settings.

■ Our model of inclusive play is informed by a number of things, the UN Convention on the Rights of the Child, the application of laws and our personal and professional values and principles.

■ An approach informed by these allows us to start to reflect on whether the children in our settings are getting as much out of their play as they might – enjoyment as well as development – and whether all the children are really included.

Further reading

Reiser, R. (2003) *Everybody In. Good Practice in the Identification and Inclusion of Disabled Children and Those with SEN: A Guide for Practitioners and Teachers.* London: Disability Equality in Education.

NPFA (National Playing Fields Association) (2000) *Best Play: What Play Provision Should Do For Children.* London: NPFA/Children's Play Council/PLAYLINK..

The value of inclusive play

Individual children and their peers, children's settings and their communities, and ultimately wider society all share the benefits of inclusive play. This chapter will look at:

- the benefits of inclusive play;

- the particular value of play to children with disabilities, children experiencing difficulties or children 'on the margins';

- short activities and exercises that staff can use in order to expand their shared understanding and knowledge of inclusive play;

- ways in which consulting children and encouraging them to express their views can be an integral part of the setting;

- how the benefits of inclusive play ripple through the community of the setting.

The benefits of inclusive play

Play itself has crucial and wide-ranging benefits to children and the people around them. This section assumes that children experiencing good quality play experiences and interesting and stimulating environments throughout their childhood will gain many benefits to their well-being, happiness and development.

This section looks in particular at the benefits of 'inclusive play' and what is gained through shared experiences of play perhaps with some support.

Children

Through experience of inclusive play in which they feel included and supported, children gain many benefits including:

- a truer understanding of the world: that there are similarities and differences between people;

- the development of attitudes such as tolerance, appreciation of difference, acceptance of perspectives and perceptions other than their own;

- a richer play environment which includes different language and methods of communication, a wider range and use of play materials;

- a positive sense of self, self-esteem and positive reinforcement of their sense of identity;

- experiences linked to curricular goals, in particular in the realms of social and emotional development, language development, knowledge and understanding of the world and citizenship;

- the ability to exercise their rights under the UN Convention on the Rights of the Child.

Children's settings

Through experiencing and supporting inclusive play, benefits gained by settings include:

- Adults and children enjoying spending time together.

- Positive relationships between children and adults in which adults show respect for the culture of children's play and in which individuals are welcomed and valued.

- Inclusive staff teams in which staff members' own life experiences, skills, languages and cultures are valued and seen as a positive resource on which the whole setting can draw.

- Reflective practitioners with deeper understanding of children's needs and the expectation that their practice should develop in order to meet the changing needs of the children.

- Practitioners with a range of skills and abilities such as varying communication skills and methods and the ability to scaffold play between children (see Chapter 4 for more details).

- A medium or 'vehicle' for delivering the curriculum which is appropriate to all the children in the setting.

- Meeting expected standards, for example principles of play in the early years (QCA, 2000: 25), and for meeting the diverse needs of children (QCA, 2000: 17), national care standards, legal requirements of non-discrimination.

The community of the setting

The community of the setting includes parents and others who have contact such as volunteers and people surrounding the setting either in the local area or through connections such as the local church, mosque or temple. Benefits gained include the following.

- Children's relationships and friendships continue outside the setting.

- Connections between children at play foster connections between parents and families through play at each other's homes and encounters in community play spaces.

- Opportunities arise for communication, building relationships and gaining a greater sense of connectedness and understanding.

- Greater openness to, and appreciation of, diversity emerges. Encounters between people of different backgrounds and circumstances or needs are based on familiarity.

- More fun and happy shared memories for all involved.

Wider society

- Greater social cohesion.

- Contributing towards aims of a fairer society in which people all have a part to play.

- More people able to actively participate in their communities in different ways.

- Meeting its obligations under the UN Convention on the Rights of the Child.

- A foundation for the future to be different.

The particular value of play to children with disabilities, children experiencing difficulties or children 'on the margins'

When considering inclusive play we often start by thinking about children who are identified as needing help because of impairment or additional support needs. However, when looking at and then developing our provision for play, it often becomes noticeable that there are children who flit around on the margins and are never really engaged in play or play with others. These children often gain enormously from improvements within the environment and opportunities for play, and when sensitive support is made available. The message from inclusive play is that it makes it better for everyone.

Play is crucial to children's experience of a setting. Whether or not the staff are pleasant, the buildings adequate, the programme varied, if the time spent at play with peers is unsatisfactory then that sets the tone for their whole view of the setting. Whether play is the primary objective of the setting or a way of working, access to play is crucial from the child's point of view. The work of hospital play specialists illustrates this well in that good medical treatment isn't enough for children to feel positive about their spells in hospital and that children's opportunities for play will aid their adjustment, coping and recovery.

Equally, play colours children's whole experience of inclusion. Child-mediated play (particularly outdoor play, playtime, free play with low levels of adult intervention) is especially important. These are the opportunities for children to have a place among peers and take part in the particular culture of play for that place. Children's play culture can have its own language, fads and phases, values, even its own history and geography.

Acceptance by peers is significant in the development of a child's sense of self and personal identity and access to that is more genuinely through play than through adult-planned activities. (We can all remember from our own childhoods how quickly children can see through well-intentioned social engineering by adults.) In play children may have to 'take on the world' – learn about relationships, how they work and are mediated – including through teasing, falling out, making up, loyalty, quarrels, shifts in groups, jealousy and so on. These are real experiences that all children have to tackle and learn about.

When discussing inclusion with children, it becomes clear that for them it centres around friendship. Friendships developed through specific attempts to provide for inclusive play are often carried over into other parts of their lives. So a friendship developed at playtime or in a playscheme has the possibility of developing into play in the children's local community or homes. These are the types of experiences that are stifled before they even have a chance to develop, when children are not able to access local play provision.

Play provokes wide-ranging language and communication and through inclusive play children will hear flexible use of language by peers including slang, word play and hilarious rude words. There is enormous motivation to use language in play and flexible use of non-verbal communication can often be more readily exchanged in the context of play. Play also offers opportunities for behaviour and traits to be appreciated in a way they might not be elsewhere – taking daring risks, making rude noises, mimicry, silliness, jokes, or telling unbelievable tales.

People and peers are a particular source of motivation, inspiration, curiosity, stimulation, and combinations of people create endlessly varied possibilities.

Many children with disabilities have few areas in their lives in which they feel able to exercise real choice and control. It may be because of change or disruption in their lives, because they spend a great deal of time having treatments or therapy, or simply because they have to rely on adults to get them around. Play can be a process through which they can regain a sense of control or work through difficult or challenging experiences. That is why play environments which have elements that can manipulated, and that can cope with processes of creation and destruction, are of great importance to children. (See Chapter 3 for more on play environments.)

Risk and challenge are integral parts of the play experience and it has been said that children with disabilities have an equal if not greater need for opportunities to take risks, since they may be denied the freedom of choice enjoyed by their non-disabled peers (Play Safety Forum, 2002). Children need opportunities in their play to learn to judge their own capacities and extend them, explore limits and to experience excitement, nervousness, courage, daring, thrills (and real spills).

Ultimately it is the nature of play that there is no right or wrong. It is therefore an arena in which children with additional support needs can be themselves, making their own meaning, gaining their own satisfaction from play in their own way and at their own pace – like everyone in an inclusive play setting will be doing.

This presents a particular challenge to adults who find it very difficult to gauge the level and type of support to provide without intruding and therefore disrupting the very dynamic they hope to support. It is this particular challenge that is a central issue in providing for inclusive play and we look at it in more detail in Chapter 4.

Short activities and exercises that staff can use in order to expand their shared understanding and knowledge of inclusive play

Even in experienced and established teams practitioners need to invigorate and refresh their ideas from time to time: the dynamics of play change with different groups of children, adults, seasons, and spaces and places to play. Practitioners with distinct professional roles may want to consider to what extent the benefits to be gained from inclusive play are within their area of concern and therefore how they see their role, with others, in providing for or supporting inclusive play (see Figure 2.1).

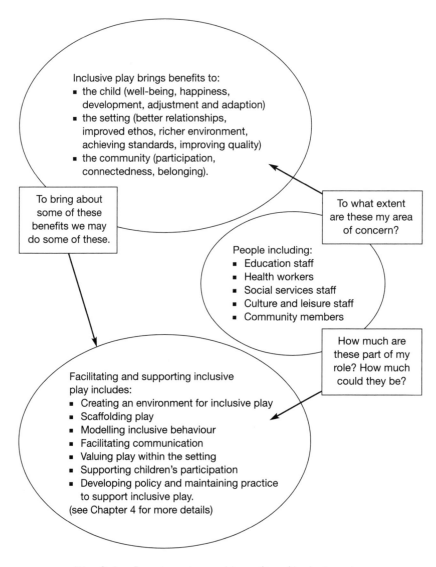

Fig. 2.1 People, roles and benefits of inclusive play.

These quick exercises are always useful.

- Swap roles: a teacher could take the place of a playground supervisor for the day; a playworker from the after school club could come into the nursery class; an occupational therapist could make playground observations. It is easy to fall into set expectations of children and ourselves. Swapping roles can give insight into children's needs, abilities and personalities in a different environment, allowing them to surprise us.

- Make a change in the environment and watch what happens. Are new possibilities opened up? Does it influence patterns of play or groupings of children? There are numerous ways to do this quickly.

  - Set up the usual equipment in different places.

  - Don't put out any equipment at all.

  - Throw a parachute over the branch of a tree.

  - Play some music from the windows.

  - Hang billows of ribbons from a doorframe.

  - Make a trail round the space with chalk, stones or shiny paper.

  - Make a stage with tables.

  - Leave out a pile of big cardboard boxes.

- Observations: spend a bit of time quietly in the play space observing the children at play as unobtrusively as possible. You could look out for different types of play, groupings of children, interactions, preferred places, preferred play materials, use of the whole space.

- Check out your observations with the children at an appropriate moment that doesn't disrupt their play. Make it positive: 'I noticed you all doing something really interesting when you were in that corner … can you tell me about it?' Children are often really keen to talk about their play provided you are genuinely interested and listening, and not seeking to intervene, direct or judge.

- Encourage other members of the team to observe play at the same or different times. Compare your observations. It is interesting how differently adults can interpret the same play situation having seen it from different angles or with different levels of involvement.

- You cannot be invisible in a play space so you may find children are curious to find out what you are up to. One useful strategy is to involve them in what you are doing. Ask them to go off and survey their friends for you on what they are doing. A little notepad and pencil in their pocket will give them a role.

The seasons, the environment and relationships between children all alter the dynamics of play.

Consulting children and encouraging them to express their views as an integral part of the setting

Listening to and consulting with children, acting on their recommendations, following up on the views that children have expressed and involving them in the ongoing processes are important in all children's settings. It may be useful to think about a culture of participation as an ongoing dialogue between all members of the community of the setting.

A culture of participation is important to the development of inclusive play in our settings. Inclusion is an ongoing process, and in inclusive play we need to make sure we are continually acting on our observations and responding to the individual needs within groupings of children.

Each child's experience is unique. For children with disabilities or additional support needs, their perception of the world and experience of it may not be like our own and we cannot act on assumptions or on assumed models of ages and stages.

We will now go on to consider the Why? Who? When? Where? How? and What? of encouraging participation (see Figure 2.2).

Why?

Consulting children and encouraging them to express their views can be an integral part of the setting and is important to the development of inclusive play opportunities.

■ Children have the right under Article 12 of the UN Convention on the Rights of the Child to express their views and for those views to be taken into account.

■ It allows us to understand the experiences of children from their points of view, and to find out more about their suggestions, solutions and perceptions.

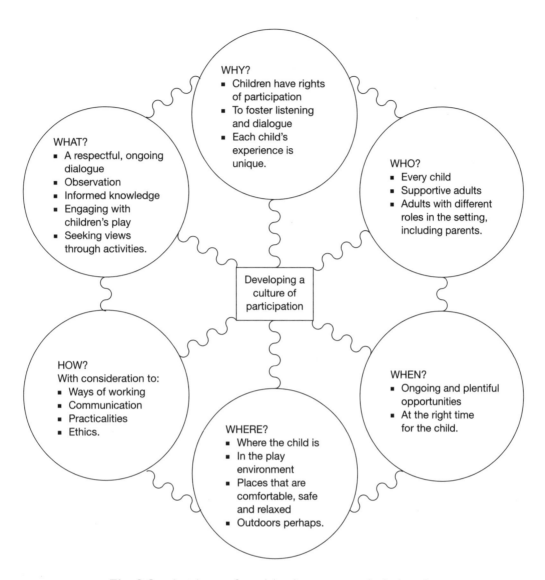

Fig. 2.2   A culture of participation supports inclusive play.

- ■ Inclusion is an ongoing process of listening to and respecting all children.

- ■ The child knows more about his or her own experience of play than an adult can.

- ■ It means we are more likely to get it right.

Playworker:	What is the best thing to do in this playground?
Child:	Splash in the puddles!

(Overheard in a children's consultation)

Who can be part of this ongoing dialogue?

- ■ All children can be enabled to contribute at a level and in a way which is appropriate to them (see below for more suggestions). The assumption should be that every child has a right to take part and express their views.

■ The participation of some children may depend to a degree on support from adults. This can include permission to participate, help with attending, support with communication or care needs. Adults closely involved with supporting the participation of children (through communication, for example) should be sure not to influence the child's views or present their own views as the child's.

■ Inclusive play is more likely to take place in inclusive settings, so the views of adults with different roles should also be taken into account and valued.

When?

■ A participative culture allows plentiful and ongoing opportunities for children to express their views. Adults will be ready to hear what children have to say (in whichever way, verbal or non-verbal, they say it).

■ Children, like all of us, need time to mull things over and form views. It can be very helpful to plan for repeat visits or consultations so that children have time to think about the issue and what they would like to say.

■ Capturing children's views often does not happen immediately. After introducing a topic children may talk about it on another occasion or talk to someone else about it (another child or adult).

■ Gaining the co-operation of other people can really help. If, for instance, parents or other practitioners know that we are actively seeking children's views, they can help to record and feed back what children tell them (bearing in mind issues of confidentiality).

■ Prior information given to the children about the subject, purpose and format of the consultation will help them to prepare.

Where?

Consulting children can take place in areas in which they already spend time and are comfortable. Although it can be great to have a consultation event in a special venue, there are also real benefits to consulting with children in their own space.

■ If the consultation is about the play environment, do it there! It makes it all less abstract.

■ In some settings, the classroom for example, children might feel that they are expected to behave or answer in a certain way.

■ It can also be useful to spend time talking with children at an event such as a picnic, during an outing or a day at the beach, when the atmosphere is informal and there is plenty of time.

■ The setting for talking to children should be conducive to feeling comfortable, safe and relaxed.

■ The sensory environment is very important, so thought should be given beforehand to acoustics, vision, accessibility, minimizing background noise and distractions.

Thinking creatively about how to consult children will help them to express their views more fully.

How?

There are a number of areas which should be considered when thinking about making a more meaningful and self-sustaining culture of participation including: communication, ethics, ways of working and practical considerations.

Communication

- Language should be appropriate to the ages, abilities and backgrounds of the particular children involved.

- Communication is not just about the spoken or written word but can involve creative methods and visual language – art, drama, music, movement. Body language, expressions and other non-verbal communication can be strong indicators of children's feelings and wishes.

- Some children use specific communication aids and systems with which the practitioner should be familiar. The child may prefer to have support from someone who is already familiar with his or her way of communicating – a sibling or carer, for example.

- Interpreters (including sign language interpreters) or bilingual support staff can be involved if children don't feel comfortable using English, remembering that they may be happy to use English in everyday situations but not be comfortable with it in a more formal situation.

- Preparing visual aids such as charts, photos and displays can aid communication considerably.

- Learning to listen to children is both an important skill and a mindset. Practise being alert to the messages children give through their behaviour, body language, their art.

Ethics – respecting children's right to participate

The ethics of children's participation is a developing area. Some issues to consider are:

- The recognition of children as competent and entitled to participate.

- Confidentiality and dealing with sensitive situations and child protection issues.

- Giving feedback to children and informing them of how their views will influence decisions.

- Genuine opportunities for children to express their feelings and opinions, taking into account their unique viewpoints and modes of expression.

- Allowing children choice throughout the process including: choice of how to be involved, of how to express themselves, of how the process might be undertaken; choice regarding where and when to participate; the opportunity to withdraw or change their minds.

- Creating a context where equal interaction can take place.

- A willingness to listen to and learn from children.

Ways of working

- Creatively (being prepared to look for and experiment with new ways of involving children).

- Flexibly (being prepared to adapt and adjust to the environment, the situation and the children's needs and interests).

- Valuing, and therefore giving time to, listening, reflection and discussion.

- Embedding children's participation in practice, ethos and policies.

- Creating clear frameworks for processes of participation (practitioners, managers, service providers and decision-makers all have roles in creating this).

What?

We have suggested that a participative culture comes from a respectful, ongoing dialogue between children and adults. It is about relationships and, at its core, about listening in all the forms that listening can take.

UNICEF (1989) suggests that:

> The Convention (on the Rights of the Child) envisages a change in relationship between adults and children. Parents, teachers, caregivers and others interacting with children are seen no longer as mere providers, protectors or advocates, but also as negotiators and facilitators. Adults are therefore expected to create spaces and promote processes designed to enable and empower children to express views, to be consulted and to influence decisions.

There are many ways to find out more about children's own experience of play and play environments. Observation of children's play is important (informed by knowledge of the children themselves, of play and of children's needs). Other suggestions include:

- Chatting to the children and asking about their likes, dislikes and preferences. Informal chatting is often very fruitful and shouldn't be overlooked as a method of consultation.

- Actively building up the children's experience of expressing themselves through creative opportunities in the setting. Always have art materials freely available for the children to use. Visit galleries, exhibitions, theatres, watch street theatre, hold workshops, stage mini-performances – all of these will help the children to build up their language of expression.

- Interviews. Develop a set of questions and interview the children or ask the children to interview each other. Using a dictaphone lends an air of authenticity to being a reporter and means the child doesn't have to be able to write replies down. A schedule of questions can be drawn up with visual prompts as well as text.

- Make a large map of the play environment and use a series of stickers to indicate areas such as: my favourite place to play, places I don't like, places I can't reach, my favourite place alone, my favourite place with friends. Give the children a set of stickers and after explaining their meaning ask them to stick them on the large map. This gives an instant visual map which you can then go on to explore more closely with children.

- Walk around the site with individual children as they complete their map. This allows more discussion about the children's preferences and their reasons for them, as you go along.

- Spending time with children in their special place allows you to explore their preferences more deeply, for example by trying to understand the sensory experiences that the child gains. These might be the sound of the wind, the flickering of light through moving leaves, the sensation of being in a little enclosed space. The children might share with you otherwise overlooked details that make the space special to them, such as a hollow in a branch, a gap in a hedge to peek through.

- Another variation is to give children a set of large symbols which they actually place around the play environment to indicate favourite places, likes/dislikes.

- The story of playtime: what playtime is like for me. Ask children for their play and play experiences as though they were telling a story. 'I went out to play and …'

Practical considerations

Practical considerations will also make a big difference to children's ability to participate in some events or activities. Areas to consider include: reimbursing the cost of travel expenses, organizing transport, whether there are constraints on the child's time, obtaining consent and ensuring that sufficient levels of support are provided.

There is a lot of information available from various organizations, websites and resources that will help to give background information and advice on all the areas covered here, for example methods of communication, participation and design for inclusion (see Useful information for some starting points).

The benefits of inclusive play ripple through the community of the setting

Once inclusive play starts to happen and people experience it working (even in small steps) it gathers momentum. People who are unsure start to see it working and recognize the benefits, which then gives motivation to keep going. Inclusive play helps all members of the setting to feel valued themselves.

Inclusive play helps families of children, who previously may have felt left out or excluded, to feel part of the setting, bringing with them their experiences, culture and knowledge. Equally, developing inclusive play can bring in these attributes from children and adults who are already part of the setting but have never previously had a chance to contribute them.

Being left out of play can be one of the first signs of a child having difficulty. Children can become increasingly isolated over time despite other attempts to include them. When play is seen as a central way in which we ensure all children feel a valued part of the setting (since it is so important to them) then it supports the feeling of connectedness in the setting.

The ethos (the disposition or character) of a setting gains much from inclusive play. Most importantly, shared experiences which are authentic, memorable and happy contribute to a shared identity which each member of the community of the setting takes with them.

SUMMARY

- ■ Children's experience both of inclusion and of play are unique and each child holds considerable knowledge and range of experience.

- ■ Participation and inclusion cannot be separated – inclusion is absolutely integral to any attempt to foster participative cultures based on children's rights.

- ■ The benefits of inclusive play are wide and long-lasting both in different and in common ways among members of the community of the setting.

Further reading

Lancaster, Y.P. (2003) *Promoting Listening to Children: The Reader*. Berkshire: Open University Press.

Shephard, C. and Treseder, P. (2002) *Participation: Spice It Up!* Cardiff: Save the Children Fund.

Creating and sustaining inclusive play environments

In this chapter we will consider:

- the influence of the environment on inclusive play;

- the qualities of an inclusive environment;

- assessing the environment for the opportunities it affords;

- improving and developing the play environment with children's participation;

- a number of steps to achieving, maintaining and sustaining an inclusive play environment.

Improving the play environment can lead to new possibilities for more inclusive play. It does not involve a direct or obtrusive intervention from adults into the children's play. Rather, it focuses on providing a platform which allows the children's own talents and interests to come to the fore and for interactions to develop naturally around the appreciation of play activity, as the following example demonstrates.

CASE STUDY

It was a rather typical school playground and though most of the children seemed happy enough most of the time some children tended to be rather isolated. Duncan was one of these children. Hoping to stimulate a wider range of play possibilities for the children, the team began to introduce loose resources such as cardboard boxes, ropes and big sheets of fabric into the play space. This is when Duncan started to display his previously unknown tent-making talent. Whenever the materials were available he was inspired to make dens and bivouacs in the playground and could ingeniously incorporate features such as the branches of the tree. His tent-making was inventive, skilful and thoroughly absorbing. Before long, of course, the other children were drawn to his activity, in which there were suddenly all sorts of exciting, new possibilities.

▶

Duncan didn't necessarily want to go on to take part in much more sociable or boisterous groups but found himself with an acknowledged role as the tent-making king, within an orbit of activity and interaction with other children.

Outdoor activities allow children to have real experiences, for example of weather, of creatures in their natural environment and of the buildings that surround them. It allows them to work on a large scale, such as in construction, water play and mapping. These experiences can be extended during indoor play, for example by looking with magnifiers at plants or creatures that have been collected carefully from the garden or making a model of buildings encountered on a journey.

(QCA, 2000: 84)

The influence of the environment on inclusive play

While the environment has a crucial role in supporting play in general, it is also an important starting point to achieving more inclusive play opportunities for children. A rich play environment creates opportunities for children to follow a number of paths through their explorations and discoveries to open-ended destinations.

A boring or neglected play environment lets children down by offering insufficient opportunities to expand and develop their play. Because poor play environments give children less chance to enjoy playing together, their play may be frustrated or destructive. This in turn can generate negative attitudes from adults who may blame the children as opposed to the understanding that the environment is failing them.

This tendency to blame the failings of the play environment on the children can lead to misdirected interventions which may compound the difficulty and further deprive children of opportunities for free, satisfying play. Typical interventions of this sort are to shorten or even abolish play and break times; to introduce more management of children's play in the form of rotas, rules, organized games, zoning of playgrounds; banning of some games.

Titman (1994) suggested that the environment conveys subtle messages to children which she described as the 'hidden curriculum'. This conveys messages and meanings to children which influence their attitude and behaviour in a variety of ways.

A poor environment, for example, may give youngsters the message that children and what they like to do are not valued enough by adults to provide something that better meets their needs. This hidden curriculum is also very relevant to inclusion. The environment and the way it is organized and labelled may convey messages to children about who is expected to use it and whether it is identified as 'special' or for everyone. For example, a sensory garden may quickly be seen as 'for' particular children.

A sense of place

It would be interesting to explore how many play spaces suggest to disabled children that 'this is a place me'.

■ Do I feel welcome?

■ Can I do the things I want to here?

■ Can I do the things I want to with my friends?

■ Do I have choices?

These types of questions can be explored with children in your own play space, by visiting other play spaces or by using photographs. Exploring these questions in situ is particularly useful as the child's response to a place can be expressed through his or her use of it (immediately zipping off to get involved or lingering at the edges waiting for help from adults, for example). This also allows questions to be asked that make sense in context and are based on the child's actual response to the environment. For example, you might ask: What made that difficult for you? You didn't seem to enjoy that much, what happened? That looked like fun, what was it like?

Children may experience the same environment in the course of their day (arriving at school, during playtime, during an outdoor lesson, at the out-of-school club) but with different expectations or restrictions placed on their behaviour there at different times. Other transitions such as moving from the reception class to Year 1, for example, may also include a change in the use of space which is implicit rather than explicit.

Some children can accommodate these differences fairly easily, while for others may find them very confusing and difficult to make sense of. It may not be immediately apparent to them what is expected of them and others in terms of roles and behaviour in a particular place. This can cause children to feel anxiety and lack of confidence in relating to others. (What am I supposed to do here? How do I join in?). This uncertainty may result in behaviour that is interpreted as difficult or challenging.

Some children need longer to make sense of their surroundings or repeated opportunities to do so. Children may have very different perceptions of the world around them or different levels of experience in interacting with it. Many children with disabilities have restricted opportunities to experiment and explore at their own pace. Therefore it should not be assumed that all children will, or should, understand the environment in the same way.

CASE STUDY

Milly made regular visits to an adventure playground. Aged 8 and with an autistic spectrum disorder, her routine for the beginning of every visit involved skirting around the outside perimeter of the space, flitting from one area to the next and spending time high on a play structure where she had a lookout point onto the playground. She seemed to need to find her bearings in this way each time in order to feel comfortable enough to try something new. The team recognized her need to do this and accommodated it by giving her plenty of space and time with distant supervision.

They planned ahead before each visit to incorporate new elements into the environment which might capture her interest. For example, one week before she arrived, they hung up a mirror and floaty scarves for her to discover near her lookout point. They watched from a distance to see her reaction. Because she liked it, the following week they added some similar sparkly scarves in a part of the playground she didn't normally go to, to see if they would interest her enough to explore a new area.

The qualities of an inclusive environment

Every play environment is made up of a unique blend of people and place. As well as physical features play spaces are made up of a certain atmosphere – an often intangible feeling of place – which can allow play to flourish in the unlikeliest settings or dwindle in what appear to be the best.

What children want from a play space varies with age, interest and circumstances. However, in general children have shown preference for places that offer variety, flexibility, natural elements, risk and challenge (Casey, 2003; Evans, 1989; Moore, 1973; Titman, 1994).

There are a number of principles which can be applied to any setting that aims to provide for play no matter what their starting point.

A very useful attempt to define what might make up a stimulating and satisfying play environment is found in *Best Play*:

Criteria for an enriched play environment:

- A varied and interesting physical environment.

- Challenge in relation to the physical environment.

- Playing with natural elements – earth, water, fire.

- Movement – for example running, jumping, rolling, climbing, and balancing.

- Manipulating natural and fabricated materials.

- Stimulation of the five senses.

34

- Experiencing change in the natural and built environment.

- Social interaction.

- Playing with identity.

- Experiencing a range of emotions.

(NPFA, 2000: 35)

The *Play Inclusive Research Report* (Casey, 2004: 27) found there are also five significant characteristics of a play environment which support inclusion:

- flexibility
- shelter
- centres of interest
- natural features
- atmosphere.

To these we will also add:

- sensory elements
- accessibility
- risk and challenge
- continuity between indoors and out.

These features combine along with an atmosphere of acceptance and permission to create the inclusive environment.

A flexible environment does not place unnecessary restrictions on children's play.

Flexibility

Flexibility requires that the play environment contains elements (loose resources, play features for which the intended use is ambiguous) which the children can use in the way, and in combinations, that they choose. There are two important points to consider:

■ that the play environment contains a variety of flexible elements;

■ that unnecessary restrictions are not placed on the children's play by an expectation that there is a right or a wrong way for the whole environment or individual elements to be used.

Adults showing active appreciation and interest in different uses of the available environment will not only learn much more about the children as individuals but will be establishing an atmosphere in which difference is accepted and welcomed. You might observe examples such as:

■ a slide being used by children to experiment with running water, for rolling balls or sliding sand;

■ a tree as a den, a 'safe' zone in tig games, a shelter for storytelling, a character in the story, a giant listening ear;

■ a plank of wood as a bridge, a river, a ramp, a shop counter, a balancing beam, a diving board, a sign;

■ a pebble and a handful of leaves as treasure, as pieces for a game of noughts and crosses drawn on the ground, as lucky charms, as pixies, as the makings of a garden.

Expectations that particular areas or equipment will be used in particular ways limit inclusive play. For some children, the commonly accepted way of using something (a slide for sliding yourself down, a house corner for playing out domestic scenes) is not immediately obvious. When they engage in shadow and light play with the reflection off the slide, or use all the kitchen paraphernalia to make patterns on the floor, they haven't got it wrong, they are not being nonsensical (although maybe that is OK too), they are just seeing things differently.

Shelter

Availability of sheltered space provides:

■ a focus for activity;

■ an alternative to spaces which cause sensory or perceptual difficulties;

■ the feeling of a safer, more manageable space;

■ privacy and a more intimate space;

■ shade from the sun and shelter from the rain and wind.

For many children the option of being in a smaller, more enclosed space rather than a very open or busy play space is very welcome. Some children are caused difficulty by particular sensory experiences, such as bright light, wind, high-pitched or sudden loud noises. Sheltered areas can be helpful to aid communication when the wind or lots of background noise in the main play space causes poor acoustics.

Centres of interest

> Findings demonstrate the significant benefits of enriching the school environment through resourcing playtime in a way which supports open-ended play around centres of interest. This allows inclusion *around* a focus, rather than emphasising the need to talk, explain or stick to rule-based games.
>
> (Casey, 2004: 27)

These 'centres of interest' in any setting allow the children to interact with them and around them. They give children the opportunity to be part of a realm of activity without necessarily having to engage directly with other children first. Becoming involved does not rely on having great social and communication skills. 'Centres of interest' can be semi-permanent, temporary or flexible features such as:

- a sensory garden
- a maze
- a paddling pool full of balls or water or lots of crinkly, shiny paper
- a sand pile with buckets and spades
- a tepee.

All of these can spark a wide range of play opportunities and play types. They provide different ways and levels at which children can choose to engage, for example contributing ideas through words or actions, following the lead of others, engaging in one's own play but within a circle of general activity, taking a turn, watching, leading, and joining in with laughter or an expressive gesture.

> The rich environment is very stimulating of play ideas. They provide focal points to meet over and something to interact around even if your play is more solitary. The den made out of a tarpaulin was a good meeting point.
>
> (Susan McIntyre, Playworker, in Casey, 2004: 27)

Centres of interest give children an easy way into a realm of play activity.

Natural features

Natural features in a play environment – trees, long grass, water, stones, logs – are an ideal way of achieving many of the benefits derived from flexibility, shelter and centres of interest. With their visual, tactile and auditory qualities, they can offer a softer and more reassuring environment than a harder built environment.

Natural elements such as shrubs and slopes help to provide shelter and soften the effects of some of the sensory difficulties children might encounter. They are useful in breaking up a wide or overwhelming space into markers that help children to locate themselves. These features can be designed to give children a feeling of privacy while in spaces that can be unobtrusively supervised from a distance.

Atmosphere of acceptance and 'the feeling of place'

The play environment is made up not just of the physical features but also of the atmosphere and this has a significant influence on how children play.

The physical environment can signal that this is a space for children, for example, through soft landscaping, scale, plenty of things to interact with. If the environment is full of signs that children have been using it – digging, interesting combinations of materials and equipment, half-built dens – there is an implicit invitation to children to use it fully. Children having their own names for areas within the environment is also a good sign that they really feel it is theirs.

Children's creative output – sculptures, paintings, planting, installations – can also be incorporated into the environment. When an environment is really working children's creativity will arise out of it: sculptures made from found objects; images made into the soil; bridges, dens, tunnels and mazes constructed.

Clear physical boundaries around the space create a sense of security. Some children spend a great deal of time with an adult shadowing them, usually because of concerns for their safety or behaviour. Secure boundaries can mean that the child can have freedom to play without a constant adult presence.

As well as developing the physical environment, therefore, the atmosphere developed between the children, between adults, and between adults and children is crucial (we will go on to consider this more closely in Chapters 4 and 6).

Sensory elements

A variety of sensory elements can easily be introduced through resourcing a play space in a flexible way with natural features. Building up layers of sensory experience will be beneficial, particularly for children with sensory impairments, and all children can benefit from the richer play and aesthetic experiences available.

Sensory elements might include:

- contrasting textures: soft, rough, uneven, prickly or tickly

- light and shade, reflections, shadows, sparkles

- subtle use of colour or gaudy combinations

- interesting noises from bells, chimes, water, things to hit, rattle or roll

- rustling, creaking, crackling and whooshing plants

- textured surfacing such as pebbles, rocks and sand.

Sensory signals can also be very useful to children as landmarks or guides. A light catching, colourful sculpture might lead the eye to an area that isn't normally much used, or whispering grasses might help children to locate themselves in a quiet garden.

Just a small area of planting can provide a world of absorbing sensory experiences.

Accessibility

Current thinking suggests that aiming to create a play space in which every element is fully accessible to every child is probably unrealistic and unhelpful. Children will not all access the play experience in the same way as each other. There can be inherent dilemmas in the aim of accessibility. For example, gates that are suitable for children using wheelchairs to open and shut can be too easy for children with autistic spectrum disorders who would benefit more from latches that are out of reach.

Rather, it is crucial that children's right to play is recognized, that they can access the experience of play as fully as possible in their own way and that unnecessary barriers, social and technical, are removed.

> Environmental barriers that exclude children with impairments, such as uneven surfaces and narrow gates, can easily be changed and are not necessarily expensive. Social barriers such as fear, embarrassment or discriminatory attitudes also need to be tackled so that an accessible play space is also an inclusive one in which disabled children and their families feel welcome. The essential ingredient for making play space accessible is a willingness to seek out and remove disabling barriers.
>
> (ODPM, 2004: 3)

For suggestions and advice see the Useful information section.

An inclusive play environment should be flexible enough to meet the play aspirations of the child (rather than the child fitting the environment). In settings in which practitioners are actively engaged with supporting children's play, a natural outcome is also to engage with the environment to help make this fit. Assumptions about children's interest and possible pursuits based on their particular impairment or condition should be avoided.

Risk and challenge in the inclusive play environment

For a number of reasons, some children have more restricted access to play that encompasses adventure, risk and challenge. In general there is a trend for children to spend less time out of doors and more time under adult supervision. Additionally some children will be affected by issues such as traffic, territorialism or racism in their area. Children with disabilities may have their access to such play limited through the lack of adequate environments, over-protection and low expectations of their abilities.

Children seek out risk and challenge in their play and benefit from it in a number of ways including:

- testing and expanding their abilities

- learning to judge risk and consequences of risk-taking

- experiencing the range of emotions associated with risk and challenge

- building confidence in their own judgements and capacity to tackle new challenges.

We must not lose sight of the important developmental role of play for children in the pursuit of the unachievable goal of absolute safety.

(Play Safety Forum, 2002: 4)

The case for introducing more adventurous elements into the play environment can be built on:

- sound knowledge of children's development needs;

- looking at the true picture of risk and safety in play environments: evidence shows that playing in a play environment is a low risk activity for children in comparison with many sports, for example (Ball, 2002);

- the positive benefits of risktaking.

We should bear in mind that 'risk' is not a fixed entity, especially when we aspire to inclusion. Riding on a two-wheeler bicycle for the first time will be as much of a challenge to some children as riding a unicycle on stilts will be to another. Climbing a scramble net is a different challenge to a child with a visual impairment than to a child with an autistic spectrum disorder.

Risk and challenge can be built into the environment as flexible elements. For example, some old tyres and planks of wood can make a ramp that gently slopes up one side and down the other or one that seesaws from one side to another, or that wobbles, or is high or low, or drops dramatically at the end for a confident biker to fly over. Children are generally very good at getting the level of risk right for themselves and tackling it when they are ready.

CASE STUDY

Children have a natural fascination with fire and a small camp fire in a play space can make a wonderful focus for cooking, singing, storytelling, role play and environmental play. However, when the inspector comes round she raises her eyebrow at the fire area in the playground. The senior playworker is ready to explain that fewer children these days have the opportunity to learn about fire safely in the natural course of the day and that it is important to introduce children to such a fundamental natural element, allowing a range of enriching experiences for the children. She explains that they use professional judgement regarding when, where and with which children they build fires. The children know what to do if there is an accident and the children are able to experience fire's magic and wonder.

Continuity between the indoor and outdoor environments

In any children's setting, it is interesting to ask whether indoor and outdoor curricula and experiences have equal status. Are they equally valued? How do we know that?

Some settings offer an easy transition from indoors to outdoors – with continuity in the atmosphere, the curriculum and expectations from one to the other. Others, because of physical design, or conscious or unconscious organizational decisions, make a clear distinction between what happens where. As this description suggests, historical factors are also an influence.

> From looking at the roots of nursery education it is apparent that that this area was initially carefully designed and laid out and its use was carefully planned on a daily basis. It was not a place to run about in after the work was done inside. It was an area in which the children were able to play for the entire session, weather permitting. It was an area where education and care went hand in hand, a wholly new concept at the beginning of the [twentieth] century. It was an area where a healthy body and mind could be developed. It was an environment in which teachers were expected to work and play with the children.
>
> (Bilton, 2002: 30)

Many children benefit greatly from easy transitions between outdoor and indoor areas to deal with stress, sensory overload, needing time away from other children, wanting to be in the vicinity of other children but not closely engaged with them, or a very real need to use their body in a more expansive way.

Children see indoor and outdoor spaces as parts of the whole environment of the setting rather than as separate domains. Maximum integration of indoor/outdoor activity and easy transitions between them facilitates the natural pattern of children's play behaviour.

Planning together for the whole environment allows us to consider:

- promoting continuously available outdoor space (in the same way as indoor space tends to be available) by organizing staff time to facilitate indoor/outdoor play and by ensuring that outdoor experiences are equally valued and resourced;

- taking the indoors out to apply in practice (cooking utensils in the sand pit, dressing up clothes and storytelling in the garden) and vice versa;

- creating direct access and planning simple solutions such as storage for outdoor shoes and clothes and having an outdoor kit for every child;

- making outdoor storage available;

- using the wider environment of streets, open spaces, parks rather than just the immediate space next to the building;

- working with the children across age-groups and across the curriculum in the outdoor environment.

Indoor and outdoor environments that are exciting, stimulating and safe promote children's development and natural curiosity to explore and learn through first hand experiences. The Foundation Phase environment should promote discovery and independence and a greater emphasis on using the outdoor environment as a resource for children's learning.

(Qualifications, Curriculum and Assessment Authority for Wales, 2004: 2)

Assessing the environment for the opportunities it affords

It is possible to expand and extend the potential of every environment to better meet the play needs and aspirations of children. Faced with an unpromising environment aspire to something better and maintain a vision of the kind of experiences that children might enjoy and from which they will benefit. An assessment or audit of the space is one of the starting points.

The audit of the environment is essentially a thorough examination, looking at the current situation, as shown in Figure 3.1. Rather than approaching it in a mechanistic manner it is helpful if we see it as an investigation in which a range of features can be explored from different perspectives, creating a rich picture. Careful observation of the space at different times as it is used by different children is very enlightening.

Values and principles, knowledge of children's play and the practitioners close knowledge of the particular children who will use the space are the touchstones of auditing the environment. By including these less tangible qualities it is more possible to achieve the aim of understanding and engaging with the space.

Asking ourselves questions about the environment will not be a one-off exercise but part of a continual process of engaging with the play space and being alert to the way children do and could use it.

There are a number of methods for carrying out the audit. Forms covering the main areas to be considered can be made up and used in conjunction with detailed observation. Ask several people to work on these at different times of the day or by covering different aspects.

Moving around the site with a simple plan on which to note details and remarks is also extremely helpful as it gives a fuller impression of the space and how it is used. Have you ever experienced the space from a perch on the branches of a tree or by peeking out from the huddle of bushes like the children do? Audits can be carried out in the context of workshops, classroom activities or a series of activities, as shown in the following example.

SAMPLE PLAY ENVIRONMENT AUDIT

This form provides space to summarize and condense information gathered through observations and other activities undertaken both by adults and by children.

Are these characteristics present in the play environment?

Characteristics and suggested details to consider	To what extent are they available in the environment? Not available (0) Minimal ★ (1) Adequate but could be improved ★★ (2) In abundance ★★★ (3)	What action is required and when?	Priority: Low? Medium? High?	Date action was taken
■ **Flexibility** – Open-ended opportunities – Varied, interesting and changing environment – Loose materials and resources – Flexibility is supported by adults	(Indicate rating plus brief notes as necessary)			

Fig. 3.1 Sample play environment audit.

© Theresa Casey, *Inclusive Play*, Paul Chapman Publishing, 2005.

Shelter – Permanent/Temporary – Child-made – Natural feature – Providing privacy	
Centres of interest – Permanent – Temporary/changing – Child-made – Natural feature	
Natural features – Trees, grass, caves, slopes, earth, fire, water – Permanent – Temporary – Available to play with and in?	
Sensory elements – Visual, tactile, auditory, etc. – Contrasts, subtlety, etc. – Permanent – Temporary	

Fig. 3.1 Continued

© Theresa Casey, *Inclusive Play*, Paul Chapman Publishing, 2005.

Risk and challenge – Permanent – Temporary – Child-made – Natural features of the physical environment	**Atmosphere** – Of warmth, welcome and acceptance – Ability to accommodate and appreciate difference – Consistent approach and framework – Signals that this is a space for children	**Access and continuity** – How children use the whole environment – Ease of movement between features – Continuity between indoors and out – Consistency of approach from adults

Fig. 3.1 Continued

© Theresa Casey, *Inclusive Play*, Paul Chapman Publishing, 2005.

■ **Surfaces**
  – Variety of surfaces
  – How they are experienced
    by the children
  – Accessibility
  – Appropriate to use		

■ **Storage**
  – Accessible
  – Secure
  – Integrated		

■ **Other**		

Fig. 3.1 Continued

© Theresa Casey, *Inclusive Play*, Paul Chapman Publishing, 2005.

What opportunities does this space afford children? What range of experience does it offer?

Opportunites and experiences	To what extent are they available in the environment? Not available (0) Minimal ★ (1) Adequate but could be improved ★★ (2) In abundance ★★★ (3)	What action is required and when?	Priority: Low? Medium? High?	Date action was taken
To have contact with nature.				
Movement – for example, running, jumping, rolling, climbing, and balancing.				
To make explorations and discoveries.				
To play without undue adult involvement.				
To interact, make changes and transform the surroundings.				

Fig. 3.1 Continued

© Theresa Casey, *Inclusive Play*, Paul Chapman Publishing, 2005.

	Details	Action required	Priority Low? Med? High?	Date action was taken?
Stimulation of language and communication.				
Social interaction. Opportunities to form friendships and build relationships.				
To experience a range of emotions.				
To play with identity (role play, fantasy, dressing up, etc.).				
In the existing environment...				
Which elements should we keep as they are?				
What should be developed, modified, repaired, recycled or re-used?				
What needs to be removed, made inaccessible or taken out of action?				

Fig. 3.1 Continued

© Theresa Casey, *Inclusive Play*, Paul Chapman Publishing, 2005.

			Comments/reminders
Are there practical issues which need to be taken into account? – Underground and overhead services – Land-use restrictions, such as rights of way – Checked with relevant authorities? – Acquired site plans?			
Setting – the effects of the weather and other environmental features on the children's use of the space (for example, shade, sunlight, outside noise which impacts).			
When should progress be reviewed?	Date		
Recommendation for another full audit?	Yes / No		

Fig. 3.1 Continued

© Theresa Casey, *Inclusive Play*, Paul Chapman Publishing, 2005.

Play Environment Workshop: an example of putting the audit into context

Aim

To allow children and adults to participate together in the redesign of the play environment.

Objectives

By the end of the workshop, both children and adults will have:

- shared experience of the value of play;
- worked together in small groups on site plans and wish lists.

Methods

- Introduction.

- Small group play activity to consider the value, the importance and benefits of play. Groups of children and adults are given some basic materials (fabric, ropes, cardboard boxes) and asked to take them out into the play space. They are asked to think about all the different ways they could play with them. Demonstrate to the other groups. Applause! In small groups think about what children gain from such experiences.

- In twos and threes, including adults and children, survey the site using ready-prepared maps and consider features that should be retained, adjusted, recycled or discarded. Encourage participants to take into account factors such as sunlight and shade or areas affected by noise from the street. Encourage the adults to listen to the children but also to participate fully with them.

- Wish lists: small group activity. Produce 'wish lists' for the space, focusing on the types of experiences and feelings they hope people will have in the play space.

- Summary of how the information gained from the workshop will be used and how the participants will be informed of progress.

Improving and developing the play environment with children's participation

Consideration should always be given at the earliest stages to the needs of the potential users. The aim is that design of the play environment, both physical and organizational, should ensure that all children can access play opportunities alongside each other.

The play space evolves in an organic fashion through the children's own play.

To encourage children's involvement in designing and organizing the play environment together, a range of methods should be available to them. Allowing these processes to develop gradually and naturally at the children's own pace will produce a more illuminating picture of the children's real needs and aspirations (Chapters 1 and 2 have already suggested some methods for doing this). The practitioners should be alert to the messages children give during informal play and chat as well as through consultation-type activities.

Here are some approaches to stimulate new ways of thinking about the space.

- Chat informally with the children. Ask them about their daydreams. Encourage flights of fancy and invention.

- Provide the children with tools, materials and loose parts to make constructions (such as huts, dens, shops) in the play space. Observe and record their ideas.

- Take the children out for trips and ask them to draw or photograph what they discover while they are there. Ask 'how can we use what we found on our trip in our own play space?'

Beginning to work towards a design

- Draw a simple map of the play area and ask the children to illustrate what they would like to do in it or how they might change it.

- The children can create models (sand trays are ideal) of their ideal play space, or older children might make models incorporating everyone's ideas.

- Use photographs of the space (or areas within it) blown up on a photocopier and ask the children to draw straight onto them to change them into the kind of space they would like to have.

Reviewing together

A period of closer engagement with the environment can lead naturally into children's participation in reviewing and considering the findings both of a play audit and of the kinds of activities suggested above. Bringing together information in an appropriate and attractive fashion that suits the needs of the children (such as displays, photographs or large scrapbooks), will help the children review and will also make a great record of the process for the future or to share with others (including potential funders).

Reviewing and prioritizing ideas and suggestions, as well as being useful learning experiences, will start to lead to the formation of a more formal design.

If particular design issues have been thrown up (such as accommodating essential services or how to go about building a play structure), people with particular expertise can be brought in to advise. This creates a wonderful opportunity for the children to be involved in identifying and understanding problems and seeking solutions. Combinations of children and adults with technical or specialist skills can result in innovative solutions from which both parties gain a great deal.

The children's play itself should help the space to evolve in an organic fashion. Play can have an immediate and direct impact on the play space through the children's activity such as digging, constructions or the building of dens.

A number of steps to achieving, maintaining and sustaining an inclusive play environment

We have now considered a play environment audit, children's participation in the process and the importance of practitioners' own knowledge and expertise. All of these will combine (as in Figure 3.2) to create a rich picture, allowing us to move on to planning and developing the play space.

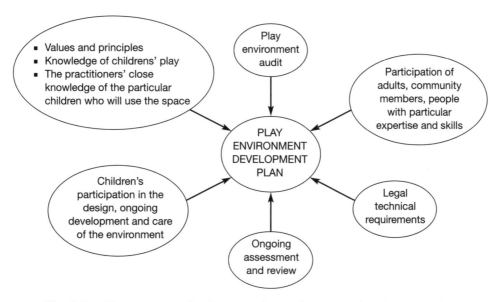

Fig. 3.2   Elements contributing to a play environment development plan.

A play environment development plan or brief will be unique to the setting, and will take into account the values and principles underpinning the process and considerations important to that particular setting. Supplemented by more detailed suggestions and ideas gathered from the process so far, the main elements of the plan may include:

- background to the setting

- values and principles

- design considerations

- methodology/process

- sources of help, advice, technical or specialist expertise and knowledge

- sources of information and resources

- sources of funding.

The plan can be revisited and revised periodically.

Policies and procedures in relation to the play environment should be based on relevant guidance, technical regulations and standards. It is vital to stay up to date with these. In the UK, the National Playing Fields Association (NPFA), the Health and Safety Executive (HSE), the Royal Society for the Prevention of Accidents (RoSPA) and the national bodies for play are good sources of information and advice (see Useful information).

SUMMARY

- Features including 'centres of interest' and flexibility, shelter, risk and challenge combine with less tangible qualities such as acceptance of difference, trust and permission to create an inclusive environment.

- Play environments are rich with potential and it is possible to give children much of the support that they need for inclusive play opportunities through the environment.

- Children's ongoing participation in designing and developing a play space over time will help to ensure that it really meets the needs of its primary users. Children can feel immense satisfaction in being involved through every stage, encouraging a real engagement and connection with the environment.

- The aspiration of an inclusive play space is not one that will have a fixed outcome. Staffed environments have the added potential to ensure an ongoing and active engagement with the space that responds to the needs and interests of the children and maximizes the learning opportunities available.

Further reading

Bilton, H. (2002) *Outdoor Play in the Early Years – Management and Innovation*. London: David Fulton Publishers.

ODPM (Office of the Deputy Prime Minister) (2004) *Developing Accessible Play Space: A Good Practice Guide*. London: Office of the Deputy Prime Minister.

Enabling inclusive play opportunities – the role of adults

The adult's role in supporting inclusive play requires a sensitive balance between allowing the children control over their own play and providing appropriate support to those children who need it. This chapter gives insight into the skills and approaches used to provide effective support to children of differing abilities together in their play. It explores:

■ overcoming fears;

■ intervention and non-intervention;

■ effective scaffolding of play between children of diverse abilities and needs;

■ facilitating communication within play;

■ modelling inclusive behaviour;

■ risk and challenge.

The role of adults in facilitating inclusive play

The previous chapter focused on the role of the environment in supporting inclusive play. The roles of the adults and the environment are crucially interrelated. The adults have an important responsibility in ensuring that the environment is a dynamic, changing and stimulating springboard for the children's play.

If we feel that a child or group of children is experiencing difficulties, we have a tendency to focus interventions directly on that particular child or group. Deciding to focus first on the way the environment influences the pattern of play and behaviour helps us to step back and to rein in that tendency.

Once attempts have been made to understand and improve the environment the role of the adult will be a great deal clearer. It may become apparent that:

- little or no additional support to specific children is necessary;

- the way to support the child's play is to build on his or her interests through suitable resourcing of the environment;

- there are specific areas in which additional support would effectively support the child.

The whole play environment is made up of everyone in it, their personalities, the weather, the seasons, events in the lives of the children and the community. We have to remember and accept that these are not all under our control. As adults working there we are an important and influential element in that whole environment – but not the only one!

The wonderful thing about bringing ourselves down to size a little is that we can also let go of some of the fears that stop us getting on with the business of grappling with inclusive play.

Overcoming fears

Enjoying the challenge of a new way of working can quite naturally go in tandem with feelings of anxiety or concern. The fears we might feel are real – but let's try and get them out of the way. Children deserve to get the best out of their experiences and our fears shouldn't be what is holding them back.

Moving forward from concerns to solutions

Aim

To identify concerns and solutions in relation to the development of inclusive play in the setting.

Objectives

- To acknowledge that our team and team members may have concerns about the development of more inclusive play in the setting.

- To give an opportunity to express these concerns and fears.

- To collectively identify solutions.

▶

Materials

■ Slips of paper, sticky tape, large sheets of paper, marker pens.

Method

■ Facilitator (may be a team member) sets the scene with a short introduction explaining where we are now in relation to inclusive play and why we have come together for this activity. Acknowledges that making change can be challenging so it is natural to feel some concern. Voicing these concerns will give us a chance to take positive steps forward.

■ In small groups, discuss and try to list issues that may create difficulties or barriers in the course of developing inclusive play. Put each issue onto a separate slip of paper. Write as many as come to mind.

■ Gather up all the slips from each group and lay them on a table or other accessible work surface. Group them together into common themes, match up any duplicates and stick them down on the left-hand side of a large sheet of paper.

■ As a group now think about where these concerns come from. The list may include things like lack of knowledge, lack of experience, myths, we heard it from someone else, we don't feel confident.

■ List these down the centre of the paper.

■ Draw arrows from each concern on the left-hand side to where it comes from (there might be several in each instance).

■ Now on the right-hand side of the paper collectively come up with suggestions to address these issues and connect up with arrows.

■ Don't worry if it ends up looking like knitting a kitten has played with! The point is to work through the issues collectively. Figure 4.1 provides an example.

■ From this activity draw up a plan with action points and time frames to address the fears and concerns.

It would also be possible to pre-prepare a list of concerns by gathering them in advance from members of the team if you feel that people would find it difficult to voice their concerns in the group.

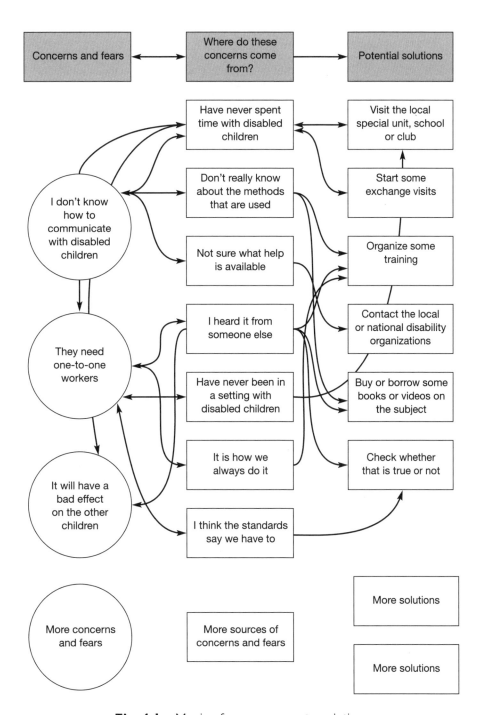

Fig. 4.1 Moving from concerns to solutions.

Fears relate to lack of experience, assumptions and myths

The most common concerns relate to lack of experience of working with children with disabilities in mixed settings, which creates lack of confidence and a fear of making mistakes. These can be addressed through opportunities to gain knowledge, skills and first-hand experience in training, through disability organizations and programmes of visits and exchange.

It is also lack of experience of working in inclusive settings which allows the myth to be perpetuated that children with disabilities will automatically require one-to-one support. There are some children who need a high level of support and should be entitled to it if it allows them to access good play experiences. However, not all children do and some only need one-to-one support for certain activities or in some environments.

Assumptions are made that children will require special and expensive equipment. Again, children who do need something specific to assist them should certainly have it; however, most children with disabilities do not need any special equipment.

Another common concern is that inclusion will have an adverse effect on the children who already attend the setting. There is firstly a worrying attitude underlying this, namely that 'our' children are entitled to attend a setting and that 'other' children can attend only if they 'fit in'. But, of course, on top of that it is just another myth, if a pervasive one. The experience of many people who have included a child with a disability in their setting is that it has had a positive effect on the ethos of the setting as a whole. Issues around acceptance, tolerance, welcome, difference and disability can be addressed directly and positively with all members of the setting's community.

Fears of loss of control

In this chapter it is proposed that for adults to support inclusive play there is sometimes a role for them to be very closely involved and to enter into the spirit of play with the children. This is suggested because it enables the adult to facilitate, scaffold and support the play in a way which it is rarely possible to do from a distant position.

Adults may accept the need to physically help a child up onto a piece of play equipment. We sometimes find it harder to join in imaginative role play when the children are in charge of the play and we are just another player (if in a complicated role of supporting inclusion by being part of the play). Some adults can become very concerned that if the children see them in this role, they will lose authority or control over the children and the situation.

This throws up a number of interesting questions including:

■ Why are we afraid of giving up control?

■ What do we think will happen?

■ If the child or children aren't in control of the play, is it still play?

In fact, there is a strong suggestion that by really entering into the spirit of play with children, at appropriate times, adults are showing children that they respect them and value what is important to them. They get to know the children better and are more able to understand their experience. Perhaps it will alter the relationship, but it will tilt the balance more towards equal partnerships.

Getting to know the children, their likes, dislikes, interests and talents will tell us more about how to support them in play than will the information of their specific impairment.

Intervention and non-intervention

A characteristic of playwork which allows children the maximum autonomy in their play, while ensuring they do not become exposed to unacceptable risks of harm, has come to be known as 'low intervention, high response' (NPFA, 2000: 16). Adults are a resource, a stimulus and a support to play but do not direct it. Adults can be available to participate in play if invited by the children.

In inclusive play we have to be especially alert to these 'invitations' to participate since they are rarely as straightforward as a verbal request. We should be alert to children's body language, facial expressions, sounds, where they choose to place themselves, what they are showing interest in – all of which can be subtle invitations for us to join them and support their participation.

Most early years practitioners would agree that if a child is absorbed in play which is clearly satisfying and rewarding, they would not want to interrupt it unnecessarily. And yet we all know of instances where children are called away from a meaningful activity of their own to complete an adult-prescribed task. This concern was voiced by Adams et al. (2004) in their report of research into the Foundation Stage in the reception class.

It is often a question of recognizing and valuing the authentic experiences that children have through engaging in play. The particular challenge for the adults in supporting inclusive play is about making very subtle judgements and interpretations. These types of decisions are about empathy and knowledge of the child, since we can only interpret but not really know what is happening when a child is at play.

A number of children are playing in the dressing up area. One of the children is sitting on the edge watching the others, playing with a hat in his hands and showing some interest indicated by his facial expressions when he watches the other children. The other children appear not to notice him. Do you intervene to try to include him?

Like the invitation to participate in play with a child, the decision of when to make an intervention to support a child's inclusion will be based on a number of things. In the example above the decision might be based on:

■ how far the child normally involves himself in this type of play;

■ his pattern of play leading up to this occasion;

■ what you know of the child's personality and preferences;

■ your relationship with the child.

Effective scaffolding of play between children of diverse abilities and needs

A very effective way to scaffold children's play to support inclusion comes from being accepted as a player alongside the children. The adult may have waited for an 'invitation' to join a group of children at play. She may be playing with a particular child who has been recognized as in need of a little extra support and may want to expand his play to enable other children to join them.

Being a participant in play enables the adult to gently hold the play together for a child or group of children when it might otherwise come apart. Children's play can be very fast-moving and dynamic. Full of verbal dexterity and in-jokes, it can twist and turn both physically and imaginatively. This can make it very difficult indeed for some children to keep up and remain with the play of the other children. Once a child drops behind, the other children caught up in their own play processes may just move on without him.

Once included as part of the play of the children, the adult can then use some strategies which will support the child's involvement with the group.

- Providing an opening for the child to join in.

- Providing a role for him.

- Modelling the play so that it is easier for the child to understand what is expected in the game.

- Pairing up with the child.

- Making the twists and turns of the game explicit so the child can keep up.

- Providing a way for the child to ease out of the play when he is ready.

There is considerable skill involved in recognizing how long to stay involved, how much to be a participant or supporter and when to slip back and forward between roles.

CASE STUDY

A group of children are playing their own imaginative game in which some children are monster-catchers, some are monsters and others are monster-sympathizers who like to help the monsters escape from their cages. The children seem to be able to change between being a monster and a catcher just by saying so. The 'cage' is a spot beside a gate.

A girl named Sunee is on the outskirts and is interested in all the comings and goings but is not joining in. The adult could use a number of strategies from within the play to support her inclusion.

- Providing an opening for her to join in: announcing, 'hey look a monster – let's go and catch it!'

- Providing a role for Sunee: suggesting a role that will suit her, maybe a monster-guard or monster-counter. Being given a simple prop may help her to identify with the role (a whistle or mask, for example).

■ Modelling the play: join in the play and characterization but stay within her vicinity and help her to understand the various characters and what they do.

■ Pairing up: 'Look at those poor monsters. We could be the escape team. Shall we help the monsters escape?'

■ Making it explicit: give short, understandable updates on what is happening and changing as the game goes along. Point out what happens at the gate/cage.

■ An opportunity to leave the play: when Sunee seems to have sustained her involvement for as long as she wants to the adult can offer the chance to join a quieter area or simply remain watching together.

Sensitive adult involvement helps to maintain children's involvement.

Techniques such as expanding, bridging and simplifying facilitate communication between children at play.

Facilitating communication within play

Children's expression of their wish to play and to play with someone else is a fundamental communication. The desire to play is recognizable without words; however, the complicated communication that happens within play can be another challenge for many children. They may need longer to absorb meaning from others, to express themselves, or may use a communication system with which the other children are not familiar. Although play can appear to be very physical in nature, communication skills underlie much of what happens. Children have to rely more heavily on verbal skill in less interesting and varied environments.

As well as using verbal communication to signal their intentions, their desire to play or their need to withdraw, in play children use:

- body language

- facial expressions

- verbal clues

- sounds

- actions.

They may also use communication systems such as Makaton, British Sign Language and symbol boards.

In play settings there is a danger that the signals children give are lost. The signals or communication may not be assertive enough or fast enough to keep up in a boisterous play situation. The other children, engrossed in the immediacy of their play, may not pick up on or understand what another child is trying to communicate and the moment is gone.

It is important to point out to children that one of their friends may need extra time and that this child has a right to be heard, but we have to remember that young children are deeply engrossed in their own play process and can easily forget in the heat of the moment to slow down or wait. Communication systems should be shared with the children in the setting – they learn fast, it can be good fun and will be an experience that stays with them. If, for example, the children have learnt the basics of signing, they can develop and maintain their own relationships without adult mediation.

Equally, one adult should not unconsciously fall into the role of the 'expert' communicator. It can happen quite easily that one adult and a child develop a relationship where they really understand each other well and so that adult is invariably called upon when a communication stumbling block arises. However, that may mean that others don't have the opportunity to develop their own communication skills or to put the time into the relationship.

CASE STUDY

Becky, who uses Makaton to aid her communication, was about to join an out-of-school care project. When the team arranged training in Makaton for themselves, they decided to broaden it out to include parents too. It was common for the children in the club to be invited to each other's houses for tea, sleepovers and birthday parties and they wanted to make sure that Becky would be included too.

The adult's role in facilitating communication in play can involve:

- expanding
- interpreting
- repeating
- simplifying
- slowing down
- bridging.

CASE STUDY

A group of children are involved in making simple 'homes' out of fabric draped over chairs and tables. It's a nice inclusive activity as the sensory elements are enjoyable and it is easy for Caitlin to join in. The children's game develops into visits between houses and knocking on doors. The child in the house either welcomes in his guests or chases them away. When Caitlin is in visitor role with a couple of friends it is easy to stay involved as she can copy what her friends do by either staying or screaming and running away. When it is her turn to be homeowner she finds it harder to know what she is supposed to do. Does she chase them or welcome them? The adult can draw on a number of ways to support communication here.

- *Expanding*: When Caitlin's friends knock on her door the adult can expand what they have communicated to an explanation: 'Oh your friends have arrived, shall we let them in or not?'

- *Interpreting*: When Caitlin excitedly pushes against the 'door', mischievous eyes shining, the adult can interpret that for her to the other children as her intention not to let them in.

▶

■ *Repeating:* When the children outside shout 'let us in!' the adult can repeat this directly to Caitlin and say, 'they said, let us in – shall we let them in?'

■ *Simplifying and slowing down:* When the children outside the door start to play up their characters, offering all sorts of reasons why they should come in, the adult can pick out the key points and repeat: 'They want to come in because they are hungry. Shall we let them in?'

■ *Bridging:* The adult realizes it is taking a bit too long for the children outside and that Caitlin's excitement shows she is ready to move on to a new stage so flings the door open and helps Caitlin into chasing mode.

Modelling inclusive behaviour

Modelling inclusive behaviour involves everyone in the setting and, when working successfully, is a reflection of an inclusive ethos. We recognize the need to model behaviour for the children but sometimes forget that they are very alert to behaviour of adults towards each other and are quick to pick up on the status, hierarchies, authority and power that are at work. In fact, this can prove fascinating to children! Adults need to be very aware of their own interactions and the respect that is given to people in different roles. One classroom assistant and playground supervisor said that no one had ever asked her opinion despite being in the playground every day with the children.

There is a certain almost intangible quality that significantly influences an atmosphere of inclusion and that is a characteristic of being interested:

■ being curious, inspired, puzzled, intrigued as part of how we respond to each other, to who we are and what we do;

■ valuing the unexpected, surprises, spontaneity, differences and detours;

■ seeing inclusion as an opportunity to learn about ourselves as well as the children.

These characteristics give children permission to play with roles and identity and to understand that people have both differences and similarities.

Modelling inclusive behaviour involves:

■ being welcoming: knowing who children are, knowing their names and how to pronounce them correctly, being interested in them as individuals;

■ accepting and valuing differences in behaviour, outlook, background and perception;

■ being a calm and consistently reliable presence;

■ being interested and enthusiastic;

■ the ability to use appropriate language and questions as an outward sign of these of attitudes and qualities.

The aim of modelling inclusive behaviour is to demonstrate these qualities and not, as is sometimes suggested, to show children how to behave in the same way.

CASE STUDY

The children are playing with bikes, trolleys and buckets of water which they are transporting back and forward from an outside tap to a moat they have dug in the sand. Some of the children have more assertive roles, leading and initiating developments in the play, but most of the children are engrossed in the mechanics of transporting the water. It is a great activity for joining in with since the busyness means there is little need to talk or explain and the purpose is clear and easy to copy. This helps Callum as he would find it difficult to play if there was need of much discussion. Once Callum has poured his bucket of water in the moat he stays to splash his fingers and drop things into it and excitedly flaps his hands up and down. Unfortunately this gets in the way of other children who are trying to fill the moat and Callum does not understand when they ask him to move so he starts to get anxious.

■ *Accepting difference*: The adult involved decides the best option is to allow Callum to continue where he is as he is obviously getting a lot from his experience, so she helps to create a new channel that the other children can pour their water into.

■ *Valuing and interested*: She digs out a hollow in the sand places, fills it with water and sitting near Callum also finds small things to drop in and observe.

■ *Enthusiastic*: The children are then given the message that Callum is doing something interesting and fun, that maybe they would like to try too.

■ *Calm and consistent*: She stays calmly nearby, showing that she doesn't consider Callum's behaviour difficult or unusual and by echoing his play gives him reassurance that his way of doing things is considered of value.

■ *Language and questions*: The adult responds to the predicament by expressing interest in Callum's activity, using positive language, rather than focusing on his anxious behaviour. 'Why don't we have a go at a new channel over here? That looks like it might work … what do you think?' 'That's a great idea Callum's trying out. I think I will try that too.'

The adult's role in supporting risk and challenge

Practitioners are in an ideal position to support risk as an essential element of play and have a responsibility to do so. They can ensure that those children whose opportunities might otherwise be restricted with potentially damaging consequences for their development, are able instead to access a healthy range of play opportunities in the setting.

As practitioners we aim to be closely in tune with the evolving capacities and interests of the children we work with, so we are well placed to take an approach that is flexible enough to respond to the direction in which the children's play is moving and to the particular combinations of children in particular environments.

CASE STUDY

The team in an environment with pre-school to primary aged children see that the older children have taken to speeding down a ramp on their bikes or scooters. The team decide that it is too risky and explain to the children that it won't be allowed because of the risk of them crashing at the bottom or knocking down smaller children. The children point out that they manage not to crash the majority of the time and they are prepared to take the chance anyway. The children and the team reach a compromise in which scooting down the ramp is allowed but only when the small children aren't around.

SUMMARY

■ In supporting inclusive play we are aiming to create the right conditions for play to flourish and, through environment, opportunities, support and atmosphere, to maximize the opportunities for children to play together.

■ Attitudes and mindsets are consistently identified as the most significant factors in the ability of adults to effectively support inclusive play. Creating an atmosphere of trust and permission, so that the children feel safe and accepted, is crucial to inclusive play.

■ Adults are a very significant, but not the only, influence and supporting factor for inclusive play. Once adults have looked at ways of going beyond fears and concerns, we are able to engage with supporting inclusive play in a number of areas and with practical strategies.

Further reading

Hughes, B. (2001) *Evolutionary Playwork and Reflective Analytic*. London: Routledge.

Play Safety Forum (2002) *Managing Risk in Play Provision: A Position Statement*. London: Children's Play Council.

Rennie, S. (2003) 'Making play work: the fundamental role of play in the development of social relationships', in Brown, F. (ed.) *Playwork: Theory and Practice*. Buckingham: Open University Press.

Inclusive play: creative input

5

A regular input of creative, stimulating resources and ideas can expand and extend inclusive play. This chapter will:

■ look at why we use creative input;

■ illustrate six tried and tested ideas for use in settings with three- to eight-year-olds:

- sensory environments

- identity, dolls, masks and dressing up

- wheeled play

- games: why and how to use them

- dens and hideaways

- outdoor art.

There are times in inclusive play when children will benefit from additional opportunities that have been chosen with a particular focus in mind, for example:

■ to build on the interests of a particular child;

■ to provide a positive shared experience for a particular group of children;

■ to nurture relationships among both the children and the adults;

■ to celebrate achievements or special days;

■ to add to the play repertoire of the children;

■ to have a really good time together.

Experiences that children and adults share together add to the collective history of a place, to the shared sense of who we are as a group.

Input for play is intended to support opportunities for inclusive and self-directed play and not to be a substitute for it. We should choose an input, wait for an appropriate time to use it, try it, stand back a little to see how it has influenced the children's own play and reflect on it again.

Resources suggested in the following inputs are intended as a starting point. Most can be gathered at little or no expense. As well as keeping the cost down, by using materials such as these we also demonstrate to children that we can adapt and appreciate everyday resources that are around us and use them creatively. Doing so demonstrates and shares environmental awareness with children and colleagues.

The Useful information section suggests a range of resources and how to obtain them.

To give all children the best opportunities for developing effectively their knowledge and understanding of the world, practitioners should give particular attention to:

- activities based on first-hand experiences that encourage exploration, observation, problem solving, prediction, critical thinking, decision making and discussion;

- an environment with a wide range of activities indoors and outdoors that stimulate children's interest and curiosity …

(QCA, 2000: 82)

Sensory environments

The aim is to transform the whole space into a new sensory experience appealing to all the senses and surrounding everyone who is in it. Creating it with the children is an integral part of the process. A sensory environment can most easily be built up within an indoor space such as a corridor, classroom or large cupboard, but it can also be developed outdoors. Choosing a broad theme helps to spark ideas to which people can contribute in different ways. Examples with plenty of scope are: the night sky, treetops, festivals, lost in space, the seashore and shipwrecks.

Value in supporting inclusive play

- Sensory environments can be particularly appealing to children with learning disabilities and sensory impairments and are accessible to all.

- Creating and using the sensory environment meets curricular goals through creative activities in a way that simultaneously meets the needs of disabled children. Experiencing them is not goal related and each individual will have his or her own unique experience.

■ They can be created quickly to inspire, amaze, intrigue and delight, or they can be developed gradually with the children to build up their involvement in a way that feels safe.

■ There is no right or wrong way to interpret, react to or interact with a sensory environment, but they do provide a backdrop to stimulate and support a wide range of play.

Planning

At the 'preparatory stage', decide on a theme, gather resources, allocate plenty of time and consider bringing in some extra help (parents, art workers).

There are three parts to the 'making stage': the backdrop, features and final details. For example, the three stages of the treetop theme could be:

■ back-drop making: creating the sky, the shape and colour of the treetops using broad sweeps to produce a quick transformation;

■ features: making nests, a kite stuck in the trees, a beautiful sun overhead;

■ details: creating eggs in the nests, magic leaves on a tree, the texture of birds' wings.

The environment should include elements that children can touch and experience. You might want to find ways for children to do this safely, for example by making:

■ sealed see-through bottles containing different combinations of liquids and small items such as marbles in washing-up liquid, pebbles in jelly, sequins in water;

■ a treasure chest, display cabinet or magic suitcase full of interesting smaller items;

■ bags containing selections that will appeal to particular children or that relate to one sensory area;

■ wall-hangings made from large sheets with see-through pockets to contain items that can be explored and then put away.

Resources

■ Materials to create quick transformation include: old sheets (can be dyed or printed by the children), a real or play parachute, netting, rolls of wallpaper, curtains.

■ Materials to make features: willow, tissue paper, tinsel, fairy lights, fabric, cardboard, spray paint, foil survival blanket (cheap, scrunchy, big and reflective), string, plenty of junk, paint, glue, big paintbrushes.

■ Materials for the final details with a variety of smells, textures, colours, sounds, tastes; natural materials such as acorns, autumn leaves, herbs, pressed petals; feathers, sequins, glitter, ribbons, buttons, corks, shiny fabrics and papers; dried beans, pasta, couscous.

Implementation and variations

■ One way to develop the theme is to build a story around it. Ask each child and adult in turn to contribute a line to the story. A starting point could be: 'One night, Joe woke up and looked out of the window into the sky full of stars. There by the furthest, brightest star he saw ...' When each person has added to the story pick out key features which can be incorporated into the environment, for example landing on a distant planet or a falling star. A child who finds it difficult to contribute verbally could contribute with the aid of a neighbouring child or adult, with a symbol or picture, or with a sound from a musical instrument.

■ When you are working on the backdrop try to cover up or incorporate obtrusive features (turn a doorway into a magic entrance to a temple) and to really make big, sweeping changes to the space.

■ Divide up tasks between the children. It is also fine for children to spend time enjoying the bustle or to move between tasks, so there is no need to get too outcome oriented.

■ The environment can be made three-dimensional with features such as paths, tents, a pond made of foil, a magic circle. Water sprayed from a clean plant spray or confetti tossed in the air give an extra dimension.

■ Vary the atmosphere with: fans to create movement and rustling sounds; lighting (try disco lights, torches, lamps, candles); slides projected onto the walls or onto banners and streamers; taped music, chimes and musical instruments; smells: essential oils, herbs, good quality air fresheners using natural oils (check whether any of the children have allergies that might be triggered).

■ The sensory environment can be used to stimulate a wide range of free play in small or large groups, storytelling, dressing up, themed games, quiet time, music, and one-to-one activities such as exploring texture, colour and sound.

Pupils who are encouraged to think creatively and independently become:

■ more interested in discovering things for themselves

■ more open to new ideas

■ keen to work with others to explore ideas

■ willing to work beyond lesson time when pursuing an idea or vision.

As a result, their pace of learning, levels of achievement and self-esteem increase.

(From the National Curriculum in Action Creativity: website: www.ncaction.org.uk/creativity)

A pupil enjoys exploring a sensory maze.

Identity, dolls, masks and dressing up

Play with identity is an important process for children and one which can and should be supported in play settings as part of continuous provision. Play with identity deals with big questions such as: Who am I? Who do I want to be? What is my place in the world? It allows children to experience different emotions, and to relate and interact in new ways. An atmosphere of permission and a culture of trust are important so that children are not inhibited by fears that they will be ridiculed or feel diminished in some way for the play that emerges.

Value in supporting inclusive play

Play around identity:

- allows children to shake off given or assumed roles (the peacemaker, the trouble-maker, the shy one);

- allows children to try out different ways of being, for example a shy child being quite fierce behind a tiger mask;

- allows children to safely try out different emotions and emotional responses;

- helps children to work through difficult or confusing experiences;

- supports a positive sense of self and identity;

- encourages children to interact in different groupings from the norm;

- supports playing around with gender roles;

- supports understanding of what different roles might be or feel like and the ability to see things from a different perspective;

- promotes understanding of the uniqueness of individuals and of difference and similarities.

73

Planning

Play with identity should be built in as part of continuous provision, but it should also be refreshed every so often to inspire the children, to highlight new resources and to follow the children's interests.

A positive outcome to this type of play is that it can encourage children to voice aspirations, concerns and questions about identity, relationships, disability or culture. Resources can act as a prompt to children and it is important that practitioners feel confident about responding positively to those in their care. Therefore, planning and preparation might include training on issues around multiculturalism, disability awareness or equality training.

Resources

- Dressing up clothes from a range of sources including some simple props that provide a role – a police officer's hat, a reflective jacket, a ball gown.

- Masks: made by the children, from different cultures, bought or borrowed ones, examples made by adults in advance, blank ones that the children can complete in their own ways.

- Pieces of fabric.

- Face paints.

- Some seating, such as floor cushions or soft chairs.

- Coat hangers and accessible storage such as a clothes rail or line.

- Mirrors: handheld, full-length, wobbly fairground-types of mirrors.

- Art materials (felt, crayons, paint mixes) in a range of skin tones.

- Puppets and dolls which reflect different ethnic, cultural or faith backgrounds and show impairment or aids such as wheelchairs, splints or hearing aids.

- Dolls and puppets made or customized by children and practitioners together to create different characters with different aspects to their stories, personalities and backgrounds.

- People: invite in guests – parents, storytellers, artists, dancers – who can talk with the children about their experiences of disability or culture, cook with them, share dance or music, teach a language, show slides.

Implementation and variations

- Truly playing with identity will happen in children's own time, so creating the atmosphere that allows it to happen is very important.

- Over-emphasizing planned activities can stifle the children's own play and start to suggest there are right ways and wrong ways to use the resources.

■ A dressing area can be effective in that children can emerge in their transformed state or experiment in privacy. It is easy to create a small area using a tent, a garden gazebo, curtains, screens or simply a circle of chairs.

■ Themed resources can be offered alongside more ambiguous materials like lengths of fabric.

■ There is no reason why the play should be confined to one area. Dressing up clothes can even be used easily in school playgrounds and create an interesting new dimension to all play situations.

■ Your collection of resources might include precious items such as a handcrafted mask, an antique puppet or a theatrical costume. It would sensible to have a special place to keep these and use them with guidelines agreed with the children.

■ Resources should be seen as part of a strategy for inclusion and multiculturalism and not simply as an answer in themselves.

■ Storytelling and use of puppets with children can help to move children's play on or to pick up on something practitioners have noticed arising in the children's play.

> Awareness of the issues surrounding disability equality and an understanding of the social rather than the medical model is essential. Resources alone do not create change.
>
> (Pettitt and Laws, 1999: 25)

Wheeled play

Play with bikes, trikes and carts is a firm favourite with children of this age group as they are learning to ride, balance, get around independently, to speed about, take corners and do tricks. All of these develop children's skills and abilities, presenting them with challenges and opportunities for essential risk-taking.

Wheeled play is a feature of lots of games that children play together – chasing, following, leading, hiding, transporting materials. It carries over into life outside the play setting as children use bikes to get around the community.

Value in supporting inclusive play

■ Wheeled play is very attractive to children in this age group.

■ Through wheeled play children can access other types of play and can easily join in group play as verbal communication skills are less important.

■ Abilities on bikes are valued among peers at this age.

- Various levels of challenge and risk-taking can be built in by the children themselves.

Planning

Building up a collection of bikes, trikes, carts and scooters doesn't have to be prohibitively expensive. Put out notices among parents, local newspapers and businesses asking for second-hand ones (in good repair). If you want to acquire specific items (tandems, two-seaters, hand-propelled trikes, for example) you may be able to borrow them from a toy library, local authority or NHS lending scheme. Trust and grant schemes may assist in buying what is required.

Aids such as footplates and backrests can be bought from catalogues (see Useful information) but some adaptations can be made quite simply, for example velcro foot straps, foam wrapped around handles to give more grip.

You will need a maintenance system for bikes. You could: recruit a volunteer to come in on a regular basis; have regular bike maintenance days when parents and volunteers are invited in (a good way to include fathers and male carers); send staff on a bike maintenance course.

Resources

- A range of two-, three- and four-wheeled bikes, trikes and carts with adapters as necessary.

- Recycled materials such as old tyres, dustbin lids, crates and wooden boards and wheels, axels, castors, ropes, and buckets from DIY stores for making homemade carts.

- Bells, horns, rattlers for spokes.

- Baskets for transporting toys around in.

- Crash helmets and knee pads as necessary.

- Dressing up clothes like police officers' hats or reflective jackets.

- Cones, planks, chalk and old tyres to make obstacle courses and ramps.

Implementation and variations

- Encourage the idea that all the bikes are for all the children to share and take turns with – there is no need to identify any as 'special'. Lots of the bikes and carts designed for children with disabilities are really attractive to all children and can be very sturdy and hardwearing.

- If the children are used to there being a variety of types of bikes, they will accept this as the norm and all the children will enjoy having different sorts to use. Some bikes or trikes are better for certain purposes than others, such as pulling things along or giving rides.

- Bicycle baskets also fit onto the front of walking frames and come in lots of funky, colourful designs.

A firm favourite, bikes and trikes allow children to join in with chasing, racing, transporting and tricks.

Games: why and how to use them

Games chosen and planned carefully can support inclusive play. There is a danger that games are used by adults as a substitute for free play when they feel that children need more support or control. However, it should be clearly understood that the benefits and experiences that children gain through organized games and free play are different, so plenty of time should always be provided for free play.

Value to inclusive play

Games can be used to:

- provide some initial structure for children who are not used to playing together or who are not used to free play;

- give practitioners an opportunity to understand the dynamics and roles within a group;

- give an opportunity for the adults and children to get to know each other;

- provide a safe routine;

- help the children feel safe and to have enough trust in the situation to go on to free play.

Planning

Gather a repertoire of games including some of the children's own. It can be a good idea for the staff team to get together first to try out games and variations to suit their children. It gives each person a chance to practise giving clear instructions and to rehearse getting past potential tricky points such as children losing interest or a few children trying to take over.

Be ready for suitable occasions to use games from the repertoire.

Teach children some games that they can play easily without an adult and use the children's own games as part of games sessions.

Settings can make up their own games book, adding to it as children and adults introduce new ideas or variations on favourites.

Resources

Most games need only a few simple resources if any – balls, strings, chalk for markings, perhaps a parachute.

Implementation and variations

- Plan a games session as an introductory session to playing together.

- Top and tail sessions with a game.

- Introduce the offer of a game at points when children start to look as if they are finding playing together difficult or if children are looking lost or anxious.

- Use a parachute or similar prop to catch the attention of children without having to overtly gather everyone together.

- Some children do need to opt out of games, finding the levels of interaction, noise or concentration difficult. There is no need to force everyone to join in and knowing the children will allow practitioners to be sensitive to their needs.

- It can be helpful to provide some easy opt-out options (such as a role as a score keeper, snack organizer or ball collector) which will then allow the child to opt back in again fairly easily when he or she is ready.

- Be aware of the environment: what are the acoustics like? Can the children see and hear the person giving instructions? Are there distracting things happening in the background?

Know the children you are playing with and adapt accordingly. Simple adaptations to make games more inclusive include:

- pairing all the children into twos, thereby allowing one child to model what is expected for another;

- seating everyone in chairs in a circle rather than sitting on the ground or standing, to include children using wheelchairs or with mobility difficulties;

- using easy-to-catch balls such as 'koosh' balls or small bean bags;

- using balls that are easy to hear or see: balls with contrasting colours, with bells or bleepers inside, for example;

- using something other than a ball, which somehow makes it less of a big deal if you catch it or not – try a lettuce, soft toy, rolled-up newspaper, a vast ball made out of a bin bag stuffed with newspaper;

- using simple props to make games clearer – the catcher wearing a hat, for example;

- making up the sequences of games in pictures, photographs or symbols to help to explain games.

There are numerous books with lists of non-competitive or 'new' games and websites devoted to games. In addition, it is possible to access short training sessions to learn new ones (see Further reading and Useful information).

A hideaway tucked into a secluded corner of the play space is full of appeal to children.

Dens and hideaways

Indoor or out, dens and hideaways are a constant source of fascination for children. Though the result might appear ramshackle to an adult eye the process of creating them is very important and absorbing. An adult-built den will probably not hold quite the same appeal.

Dens stimulate a range of play, offering experiences that are quiet and reflective through to those that are thrilling and daring.

If it is not possible to simply let children locate their dens wherever they choose, it should be possible to identify an underused area of ground where children can get down to some serious den-building – areas in bushes and among trees are always appealing.

Value in supporting inclusive play

- Dens provide a centre of interest for children to interact with and around.

- Children can easily make dens themselves from a range of materials and at different levels of complexity.

- Children's den-building easily grows into community-building with a series of dens becoming a village or a series of settlements.

- It stimulates communal play involving visits to each other's dens, chasing away, hiding, inviting in for secret plans.

- Dens provide an alternative calm space for children who feel stressed or anxious.

- They offer the possibility of shelter and privacy.

Planning

Resources for dens are easily gathered. Ideas for variations on dens can be stimulated by looking at types of shelters and dwellings from around the world, from different periods of history, from different species of animals, and by reading stories that feature safe havens, nests, castles, caves, igloos, hermits.

Thinking through and planning for health and safety issues may influence the type of resources required. For example, should dens be packed away at the end of the day or can they be left out? Remember to balance the intrinsic value of the activity with any perceived risks.

Resources

- Natural materials: branches, tree stumps, logs, willow, stones, ice, bales of hay.

- Semi-permanent/outdoors: tools, wood, ropes, tyres, tarpaulins, paint.

- Indoor/temporary: fabric, blankets, cushions, clothes airer, table, stools, golf umbrellas, large cardboard boxes, poles.

- Props such as table cloths, picnic sets, hard hats, broomsticks, dressing up clothes, torches.

Implementation and variations

- Be cautious not to encourage den-making opportunities that will by their nature exclude (dens in very inaccessible spaces, for example), but at the same time remember that a tree house might be especially thrilling to a child who is usually earth-bound.

- Sometimes entry to dens is linked to the membership of a group so practitioners may need to stay alert to how they are being used. But act with some caution. Insisting on particular children being included probably won't help. Issues about exclusion can be discussed elsewhere.

- Helping some children to create dens themselves and using them as a focus of activity may help.

- Den-building indoors is also full of possibilities – from the classic den made from a clothes airer and a few blankets to more elaborate creations making caves from papier mâché, tepees from poles and fabrics.

- Dens and hideaways are great for free play, storytelling, private conversations, for quiet time, relaxation, for massage, adventure.

> The children came running in saying "Mr Howe, come and take some photographs".
> I went out and the children were building a bark-age village.
>
> (Sandy Howe, Head Teacher)

Outdoor art

Play in outdoor environments gives rise to spontaneous expressions of creativity from children. The outdoor environment provides children with opportunities in their play for manipulating real materials; for experimenting with found materials; for exploring the nature and quality of textures and colour; and for experiencing the effects of light, change and transformation. Art and creativity can be supported in the outdoors through the introduction of techniques, methods and frameworks of ideas to the children.

Value in supporting inclusive play

- Using found materials in the outdoors frees us from the limitations and expectations sometimes imposed on specific materials in indoor art settings and from the notion that there are 'those who are good at art' and 'those who are not'.

- Every creation in the outdoors using found, natural materials is by its nature unique and tends to be quite ambiguous. It doesn't have to be representational and so allows for personal interpretations.

- Taking part in outdoor art and also finding evidence of it around the play environment reinforces an ethos of accepting and valuing different ways of being and doing and signals that this is a space for children.

- Outdoor art allows children to experience creation and transformation, decay and destruction.

- It gives children a chance to become more aware and in tune with the natural world, the change in the seasons, the effects of light and weather.

Planning

Develop a shared understanding that the outdoor environment is there to be used by the children. Explore the space with the children and identify areas that would be conducive to outdoor art. Think about specific ways to introduce art into the outdoors and how you might resource that.

Plan for different inputs at different times, but continuously allow for children's own creative interactions with the outdoor environment.

Resources

- Natural materials: driftwood, grass, sand, water, willow, a nest, moss.

- Found objects which can be gathered and introduced into sculptures or mosaics: tiles, old wheels, beads, bits of crockery, broken toys and cement, plaster, chicken wire.

- Mark-makers: rollers, paintbrushes, sticks, charcoal, sponges, mops, straws, halved-potatoes, stones, wheels, hands and feet. (Chunks of foam tied onto lengths of dowelling make good long-handled tools for mark-making; wrapping bubble wrap or foam around the handles of paintbrushes or rollers can make them easier to grip.)

- Easels, buckets of water, paint, wallpaper, cardboard boxes, glue, wallpaper paste (without fungicide), chalk and biodegradable powders such as flour for making trails.

- Polished pebbles, feathers, shiny papers, dried slices of oranges, lemons and limes.

- Snow, ice, rain, reflections, shadows, ripples.

The play of sunlight and shadows enhances the experience of drawing outdoors.

Implementation and variations

Outdoor art activities are very, very simple to introduce.

- Take big cardboard boxes outdoors and paint them.

- Draw a big picture frame in chalk on the ground and leave out the chalk for the children to get on with.

- Staple long pieces of paper to the fence and provide paint and mark-makers.

- Stretch a plastic sheet or shower curtain between two points. The children can paint on both sides, see through it and see the effect of light.

- Cover the children from head to toe in boiler suits and let them splash paint onto the ground or onto very large sheets of paper or fabric.

- Make wild patterns by letting the children stand in the large trays of paint wearing Wellington boots or just bare feet then dance around on a large sheets of paper or fabric.

- Make track patterns with the wheels of bikes or wheelchairs coated in water-soluble paint.

Ephemeral art

- Use autumn leaves and grasses to weave through wire fences to create patterns. Leave them as they gradually disintegrate naturally.

- Create patterns with pebbles in puddles. See how they change as the puddle dries.

- Match the colours of leaves and create a pile of each to use as a 'palette' to make pictures on the ground.

- Throw a bundle of leaves into the air and dance in them as they fall.

- Make a frame out of pebbles or twigs on the ground and create collages within them.

- Give the children an instant camera to capture beautiful effects that they find – raindrops on leaves, the sun sparkling through a cobweb, sharp contrasts of light and dark. Make a montage from these pictures.

- Paint with large brushes and buckets of plain water.

Art objects integrated with the environment

- Look for nooks and crannies in walls or shrubbery to contain small artworks.

- Make easy sculptures from small pieces of wood nailed together onto a flat piece about A4 size and coloured with wood stain. Hang up around the area.

- Paint smooth stones with colours or patterns, varnish and use to make trails or magic circles.

- Bring in an artist to work with the children to create sculptures, mosaics, murals.

■ Look for inspiration from: the materials themselves, the sky, the light, reflections, sensations, how you feel, what you see and hear, cobwebs, rainbows, shadows, changing seasons, your breath in the air, autumn bonfires, crunchy frost, soggy grass.

A water sculpture integrates art, play and nature.

I found I could say things with color and shapes that I couldn't say any other way … things I had no words for.

(Georgia O'Keeffe, twentieth-century American artist)

SUMMARY

■ There are times in inclusive play when children will benefit from additional opportunities that have been chosen with a particular focus in mind.

■ Thinking through the reasons for particular inputs, based on your observations of the children at play, allows you to assess the effectiveness of that input and to plan for any further support to inclusive play.

■ Creative input for play is intended to support opportunities for inclusive and self-directed play and not to be a substitute for it.

■ Look for inspiration all around you by keeping an eye open, stealing ideas, browsing on the Internet, signing up for courses. You can find inspiration in: the materials themselves, the children, what they do and who they are, the light, sensations, how you feel, cobwebs, shadows, changing seasons, your breath in the air, autumn bonfires, springtime planting.

Further reading

Cooper, V. and Blake, S. (2004) *Play, Creativity and Emotional and Social Development – Spotlight Briefing*. London: National Children's Bureau.

Marl, K. (1999) *Accessible Games Book*. London: Jessica Kingsley Publishers.

Murray, D. (2004) *Pick & Mix: A Selection of Inclusive Games and Activities*. London: Kidsactive.

Pettitt, B. and Laws, S. (1999) *It's Difficult To Do Dolls: Images of Disability in Children's Playthings*. London: Save the Children/Action for Leisure.

Working together

If inclusive play is to become a regular, natural part of the setting then it is vital that staff and other adults work together. This chapter will provide some advice and guidance on useful approaches to planning for inclusive play and involving people in various ways to achieve it. It looks at:

■ planning for inclusive play: redefining roles for adults, finding ways to make it work, supportive structures for children;

■ observations and documentation;

■ involving people.

Planning for inclusive play

Underlying successful approaches to inclusion is the recognition that everyone in the community of a setting shares responsibility for it. Although it is often assumed that inclusion requires extra staff, or that the children with disabilities will need one-to-one assistance, very often that is not the case. The general principle to bear in mind, however, is that any additional staff should be integrated in the team and that inclusion remains a shared responsibility.

A review of the role of adults in the setting, questioning and reflecting on current practice, can be a useful basis for planning and reorganizing in order to facilitate more inclusive play. As Figure 6.1 shows the views of adults and children can be brought together by asking questions about current and potential roles.

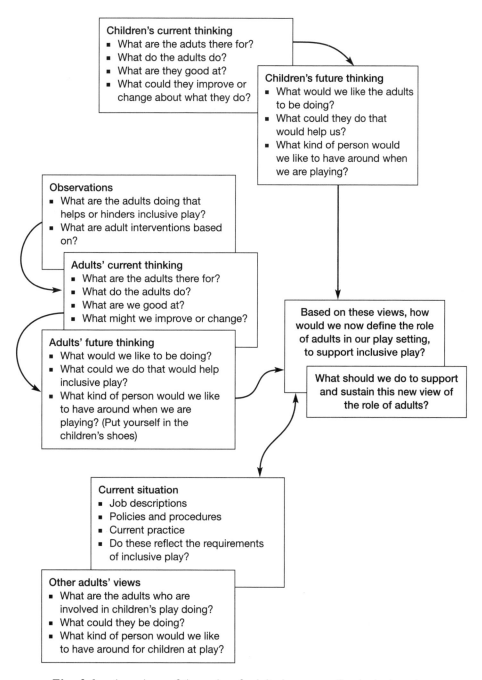

Fig. 6.1 A review of the role of adults in supporting inclusive play.

These questions can be asked of children in different ways. For example:

■ A 'small world' model of the setting, showing indoor and outdoor space, can be made using simple drawings or symbols to identify different areas that children use. Small play figures can be given to the children to represent how they see the role of adults. The practitioner can use questions to prompt the children about how they see or would like to see the role of adults. The discussion can be recorded using a tape and video recorder, notes or photographs with the children's permission.

■ Lay a large piece of paper on the floor and draw around an adult to create a life-size figure. The children can draw or write their thoughts about the role of adults onto this. Again, prompt questions will be useful and an adult may need to capture some of the views of children that are spoken but not written down.

■ Take lots of photographs of adults and children doing things together in the course of a few play sessions (perhaps in different weather or when there are different play opportunities on offer). Use these photographs to sort and discuss in small groups.

Adults may find these activities rather intimidating, so it is important that the team has discussed the purpose and method together and see it as a constructive way to gain feedback for the whole team. Equally, children will only really express their views if they know they are being listened to and their reviews respected. They should be told how the views they express will be used and how they will receive feedback. If the children express views that the team find challenging, it is important that those views are not suppressed. It may be a useful strategy to explain to the children that a particular comment or suggestion will be discussed further and that someone will get back to them.

The views of both children and adults can be sought and brought together.

Questions asked among the adults can utilize observations made during play. These observations may have considered how the adults' actions help or hinder inclusive play and what the basis of interventions appears to be. Are interventions often prompted by adult concerns about noise levels or rough and tumble play? Are they focused on children who stand out for some reason? Are they prompted by children appearing to need help? Are they proactive or reactive? Are they responses to invitations to play from the children? (You may find it useful to look back to the skills and approaches described in Chapter 4.)

To complete this gathering of information, it is useful to look at policies, procedures and job descriptions that have a bearing on play, and consider whether they really reflect the requirements of inclusive play.

This gathering together of views and perceptions about current and potential roles leads to two consolidating questions:

How would we now define the role of adults in supporting inclusive play in our setting?

What should we do to support and sustain this new view of the role of adults?

Finding ways to make it work

Having redefined the role of adults the team may need to consider ways of working that will support the aspirations for play in the setting. Most important, and often in short supply, is time for the team to reflect on practice and plan together on a daily basis. A refreshed look at the role of adults may suggest the need to free up some time for adults to engage more directly in play or the need to facilitate continuity between indoors and out, for example.

Possible solutions may include:

Improving the environment so that children have more opportunity for satisfying play, which will allow adults to move from supervising to facilitating.

Considering whether it is possible to free up even small amounts of time to allow for setting up and resourcing the play space before children use it. This time will be repaid doubly by the change in the way in which the children play.

Sharing responsibility for tasks such as gathering resources, making creative inputs, improving the environment and involving other people. These tasks can be designated to members of the team and rotated regularly.

Considering how members of the team are positioned around the whole provision during free play. Each setting is different but variations to try are:

– Locating staff in key areas but allowing children free flow between them.

– Allowing staff and children fluid movement around the space but with a clear awareness among the team that there will always be a certain number of staff indoors and outdoors at any one time.

– Locating a number of team members at key areas but arranging for some members of the team to 'float'.

– Having a good look at the space to identify points that make it easy for adults to supervise unobtrusively.

– Team working and ongoing communication will allow movement around the space that supports the children's play. If a child and adult are deeply engaged with one another in play that moves around the play space, it would not make sense to rigidly stick to artificial divisions of space, providing all members of the team have a clear understanding of what is agreed and required.

89

- If the norm is for children to be divided into groups by age or in any other way, consider bringing them together with the adults working with them in a team style.

■ Most important is making and protecting time to spend together reflecting and planning.

Supportive (but not limiting) structures for children

Like adults, children may need a supportive structure around their activity that allows them to feel safe and secure in what they are doing. These supportive structures might be physical, such as boundaries, but often also include other types of support. Some children with disabilities may find it particularly helpful to have a structure that is easy to understand and that allows them to frame up what is expected.

Possible supportive mechanisms include:

■ picture timetables made up to indicate the sequence of the day, for example bus, welcome, play, coming together for a snack, play, goodbye song, bus;

■ reliable routines such as: a warm welcome from known staff; familiar play equipment in the same place as well as anything new or rearranged; quiet calming music played at lunch and snack times; a quiet space available to 'escape' to; a reminder when it is nearly time to finish up; a final gathering together; a review of what happened that day and goodbyes;

■ transitions between places and activities that make sense to children, for example one group of schoolchildren who attended an adventure playground weekly found the bus journey a useful transition from school mode to play mode;

■ pairing or 'buddy' schemes when each child is matched with a buddy who can look out for and support them;

■ de-cluttering of the space so that it is not overwhelming or too confusing;

■ a reliable presence and consistent approach from all the adults in the setting.

Observations and documentation

Observation of children's play is crucial to understanding and planning effectively for inclusive play. Observations also serve to develop shared understandings within teams and as a basis for dialogue within teams and with parents and children.

Making observations and recording them only makes sense if this information will be used in some way. Observations can take many forms and it may be appropriate for a team to use one method for a period of time and then to use another. Methods might include:

■ Team discussions at the end of a play session, where the perspectives of each member of the team are gathered. This has the benefit of providing an overview of the session, to highlight different interpretations of the same incidents and to allow a whole picture to unfold of a sequence of events that might not otherwise be apparent. This method also allows for more experienced staff to pass on knowledge and skills and for shared understanding to develop that enhances the ethos of a setting. It provides opportunities for a team to problem-solve and to make collective decisions about future actions. A simple format can help to focus a discussion, such as the example shown in Figure 6.2. Alternative formats might be more general or prompt the team to think about other questions such as what the children gained from the session, the role of adults, what helped or hindered inclusive play. The team may choose to have a particular focus for a period of time and then change it once it has been explored in some depth.

■ The team may decide to focus observation on particular children on a rotating basis. For example, all staff for one day record observations of Jade and Abdul each time they spend time in the same area as that person. At the end of the day a number of observations by different adults can be brought together. Through this targeted method a detailed picture of the play of particular children on a particular day can be built up, generating suggestions for extending, supporting or enhancing the child's experience. It may be appropriate to go back to the child or children and check out with them any hypothesis that arose since adults' view of children's play is only by nature an interpretation. For example, a teacher felt that a session in which a child was intent on making a den which was constantly being raided by another child was unsuccessful because of the conflict arising between the children. When she checked with the children it seemed there was an implicit invitation in the den-building to provoke a raid by the other child.

■ Video and photography can also be used (with the children's permission) to make observations of children that can be reviewed and discussed in detail with colleagues or parents. Recordings may focus on particular areas (for example, sand and water), particular types of play (for example, imaginative and fantasy play) or on particular children.

Documentation adds another layer to observation, making visible the processes we observe taking place. If documentation is displayed, integrated into the environment and shared with the children and other adults, the process can in itself become part of the character of the environment and an investigative atmosphere.

Documentation shows children that their play is taken seriously. It provides a basis for dialogue and for developing shared language and understanding with other practitioners and with parents and children.

Documentation of what happens in a play space over a period of time gives value to the time that children and adults have spent together. It creates a visible history – the story of the place and time together. It contributes to the 'remember when' factor that helps to build a sense of community. It provides individuals and groups of children with an opportunity to revisit and reflect on past experiences.

Sample daily observation sheet	
Date	Number of children attending (see register)
Members of the team involved in the session (staff and volunteers)	
Notes regarding any particular feature or focus planned for the day (e.g. planned creative input, visitors, new child arriving)	

What types of play did the children experience in this session?

What were the influences on the children's play experience, both positive and negative? (e.g. weather, seasons, adults, resources, etc.)

What was the most significant moment/feature of this session? Why?

What could we have done that would have improved this session?

Feedback from children or visiting adults:

Action points:

■

■

■

■   (continue overleaf as necessary)

Fig. 6.2 Sample daily observation sheet.

© Theresa Casey, *Inclusive Play*, Paul Chapman Publishing, 2005.

Methods include:

- video taken with a focus in mind (one child, a type of play, one area of the setting, adult practice) and used as a basis for discussion and reflection;

- laminated photographs and captions, made into sequences, books or displays;

- scrapbooks of periods of time, events or projects;

- collections of objects and children's art together with captions using the children's words or adult's notes to contextualize them;

- display boards and stands;

- photographs taken by children or adults, assembled to illuminate children's perspectives or processes taking place.

These need not be additional tasks tacked onto the busy day but can be seen as a way of sharing in the experience with the children and working with them to make sense of what happens around and between them.

Involving people

Supporting inclusive play can involve a number of people both from within the setting and in the extended network. Depending on the context of the setting teams may want to involve families of the children (including grandparents, carers, siblings), colleagues from other settings or with a range of professional roles (health or social workers, physical activity co-ordinators, inclusion officers), volunteers, students and trainees. They may want to make links between settings (the school and the after school club, a mainstream and a special school) or between services (play and health, community development or social work).

All of this takes time and planning, but fostering involvement contributes both to the sustainability and to the effectiveness of support to inclusive play. There are numerous reasons for developing involvement including:

- the potential to bring into our settings the benefits of diverse skills, cultures, backgrounds, experience and language;

- to develop a sense of community around the setting;

- to get things done;

- to keep ideas and skills fresh;

- contributing to an ethos in which our settings are proactive and outward looking;

- having a relationship with the family which affords us better understanding of the children;

■ children having contact with a diversity of adults and families, helping them to understand that there are different models of families, different cultures and ways of doing things.

Involving people includes, of course, ensuring that disabled people as parents, volunteers, colleagues and members of the team have the same opportunities as others to contribute their skills, experience and knowledge and to participate in the development of inclusive play in the setting.

Simple strategies to support inclusion in participation

■ Ask the person what would make it easier for them to become involved and any specific assistance that would be beneficial.

■ Ensure that any information provided is in large print if on paper, free of jargon and available in a suitable range of formats or languages, for example Braille, audiotape, or video-taped signed information. Find out if the local authority or voluntary organization has a translation or interpretation service.

■ Nowadays, many children's settings produce much of their own information using word-processing packages which make it very easy to produce information in preferred colours, type-size and font.

■ Don't forget the importance of face-to-face communication, for example taking the opportunity to talk when parents pick up and drop off children.

■ Be proactive about ensuring the physical accessibility of the setting, about challenging assumptions on the lives of disabled people and about accessing information that can help (see Useful information).

There are a number of areas in which people or organizations can be involved in supporting inclusive play at varying levels, from direct work with children and hands-on development of the environment through to joining management committees or assisting with development of the skills and knowledge base of the team. Possible areas to develop involvement in inclusive play include:

■ play environment design;

■ creative inputs to play;

■ gathering resources;

■ practical help such as bike maintenance, gardening and building play equipment or structures;

■ play with children;

■ assisting with photography, video or with the layout and design of leaflets and posters;

■ raising awareness of the issues around play and inclusion;

- developing links between services and settings;

- contributing experience, knowledge and skills such as communication skills, consultation techniques, play theory or playwork approaches.

The right of every child to play is an issue that most people recognize as being of great importance and which it is possible to galvanise support for. But because it is also rather taken for granted, we may need some strategies up our sleeves to involve people and then to keep them motivated.

Strategies to help people connect with the issue

- Highlight the importance of play in documents, leaflets, posters used by the setting.

- Give presentations to parents or colleagues focusing on play and its benefits.

- Help the children to develop presentations or presentation materials about play in their lives: what and where they play, who they play with, how they feel about their opportunities for play.

- Assist the children to organize tours in which they lead adults through their play environment pointing out key features and issues. The children should be given plenty of time to plan and think this through in advance. They might like to have prompt cards with words or images in key places to remind them what they want to emphasize.

- Undertake consultations with children with disabilities or additional support needs and their families to find out about the range of play opportunities (if any) that are available to them.

- Use workshops to highlight the importance of play, inclusion and the right to play (use activities suggested in Chapter 1).

- Include colleagues from across traditional professional boundaries in sharing understanding of inclusive play and identifying how their roles connect both with play and with each other's roles.

Strategies to keep people motivated

- Use a participatory approach to development so that everyone has the opportunity to contribute.

- Highlight the connection between the contribution made and the ultimate benefit to the children, for example showing how the children made use of resources, examining 'before and after' pictures of a play environment, using case studies from the team which illustrate how they have used ideas gained from training input.

- Recognize contributions, achievements or progress in a range of ways: being welcoming and saying thank you; providing expenses and refreshments; acknowledging contributions in reports and meetings; sending thankyou cards and letters; taking photographs and making displays.

- Ensure that all members of the team, including volunteers and students, are able to take part in team discussion and reflections.

- Arrange external opportunities such as study visits to other play settings, attending conferences and meetings which volunteers, parents and others can attend as well as staff team members.

- Bring in expertise from play organizations, trainers, specialist workers, arts workers to work alongside the team collaboratively.

Try it

Sometimes the best way to help change happen is to get on and try it. Practitioners with a range of roles may like to try working together to:

- arrange and facilitate a play session or event based on simple resources;

- allocate a short time frame and designate small groups to focus on developing some play opportunities based on different types of play and report back;

- ask each person to bring an example involving inclusion and play from their own setting/profession and discuss;

- ask each person for examples of how they could build inclusive play into their role/provision;

- for each of the above, consider as a team or across professional roles how you can help each other to achieve more inclusive play.

SUMMARY

- The general principle is that inclusion remains a responsibility shared by all members of the community of the setting.

- Adults should be solution-focused and their ways of working flexible enough to help inclusive play happen.

- Observation helps us to understand better children's play and the meaning-making within it, allowing us to facilitate more effectively.

- Fostering involvement contributes to the sustainability and effectiveness of the support we give to inclusive play.

Further reading

Clark, A. (2004) *Why and How we Listen to Young Children*. London: National Children's Bureau.

Dickens, M. (2004) *Listening to Young Disabled Children*. London: National Children's Bureau.

Both of the above are from the 'Listening as a Way of Life' series of leaflets.

Managing for inclusive play

Inclusive play flourishes more readily in settings with a genuine ethos of inclusion; settings in which people and relationships are valued, and given time and attention.
In this chapter we will look at:

- ethos

- changing attitudes

- creating a framework to support inclusive play

- writing a play strategy.

Ethos

The ethos of a setting – the distinctive character and spirit that make it what it is – is evident throughout the practice and relationships within the setting. Ethos evolves from our values and beliefs but is also very much about putting them into practice as it affects the decisions we make, what we do and how we behave towards each other.

Inclusive play is more likely to happen in settings with an inclusive ethos; settings in which positive and respectful relationships are modelled, recognized and supported. The ethos of a setting is not static but is sustained through the efforts of individuals and the extended community of the setting. A general disposition towards inclusion will result in more of the features that support inclusive play (attitudes, environment, behaviour, shared goals) being in place.

In managing for inclusive play, then, the ethos that pervades the setting will be a great influence on the outcomes for children. Does it result in a welcoming and supportive atmosphere; a disposition towards problem-solving; a willingness to give things a go; the removal of disabling barriers?

The habits found in an ethos that is supportive of inclusive play might include:

- giving time and attention to communication and relationships;

- valuing people with all their differences and similarities;

- finding and giving opportunities for everyone to contribute their views, personalities, skills and ideas;

- supporting a sense of belonging;

- valuing play highly and demonstrating that we value it through actions that support it;

- a playful disposition.

Team activity: inclusive habits

Observe the interaction of the team over the course of a few days and note down some of the 'habits' that you observe. For example, faced with a challenge how does the team tend to respond? Is their response generally to find a way to eliminate the problem as quickly as possible? Do they look at it from different angles and come to a rounded view? Do they like to see challenges as an opportunity? When children come up with different ways of doing things are they allowed to follow their own path or do adults think it is more important to keep them on track using planned activities?

These observations can be discussed in a feedback session. Do our aspirations for inclusion and our observations of what actually happens match up? What might need to change and how could we go about that?

To manage for inclusive play we need a strong sense of what we are trying to achieve and the ability to create a framework in which it can happen and continue to develop.

Team leaders and senior practitioners need the ability to articulate the values and principles of inclusive play both within the setting and externally. A robust understanding of the issues around inclusive play should be developed throughout the setting and needs strong support from the team leader, so that practitioners feel confident in their own professional judgement.

There are many occasions when we need to be able to state the case for play and the basis of our judgements, for example being able to explain the benefits of rough and tumble play, the importance of risk, why it is fine to play in the rain, why play with gender is not considered a problem.

The team leader will demonstrate commitment to inclusion and children's participation in their own actions and through policies and codes of practice. They need to have a good grip on what needs to be done to work towards inclusion in the setting, and to be able to identify priorities, action and progress.

MANAGING FOR INCLUSIVE PLAY

Leadership styles evolve with experience and each individual will have their own style reflecting their personality, which draws on their strengths and the strengths of the team. Each leader will find his or her own balance of the role in supporting inclusive play, managing tasks, fostering relationships, working with the team and working with the particular context of the setting.

Listening, giving praise, acknowledging and valuing contributions of different sorts, asking for input and help with problem-solving will all play a part in developing an inclusive approach.

Changing attitudes

Attitudes are consistently cited as what makes the difference in inclusive provision. Working towards more inclusive play in our children's settings therefore implies that we have to give time and attention to attitudinal change.

Changing attitudes is not always easy but there are some strategies that can be useful.

- Before we can change our beliefs or our practice we sometimes have to let go of a previously strongly held view or idea. It might be something into which we have put time, energy and commitment, for example developing a particular type of provision, advocating the need for specialist services or believing what we do is good enough already. Spending time finding out about these 'prior commitments' and talking them through can start to allow space for change.

- The advocate for change can show empathy with the loss that the person might feel. Make genuine attempts to listen to and understand the other person's point of view.

- Change happens in stages, steps back, forwards and sideways. We probably wouldn't have arrived at the stage we are at now without the previous ones, just as where we are now is not a final destination. One day people may take inclusion so much for granted that they will look back and wonder why we were struggling so much in our efforts to make inclusion happen.

- People should be provided with the opportunity and information to recognize the need for change and the time to accommodate new ideas. Giving information, opportunities for visits, conversations with children and adults with disabilities, and attending conferences may assist shifts in thinking.

- Not changing is also a choice with its own benefits and dangers. What happens if we just carry on doing what we do regardless of the changing climate of inclusion or the policy and legal context? When looking at the reasons for change we needn't be afraid of also examining the consequences of not changing.

- Identifying people whose influence carries some weight and bringing them in to share their views can be extremely useful. These might be parents of children with disabilities, disabled adults, colleagues from other settings, academics. If putting people together in person is difficult then magazine articles, academic papers or videoed discussions or lectures might help.

■ Try to harness the energy that is put into resisting change and redirect it – perhaps by asking the person to lead a subgroup, take on a policy review, gather information. Involvement in the process of defining goals and working out how to reach them will be more motivating than feeling only an external pressure to change.

■ One of the most powerful ways of changing people's attitudes to inclusive play is for them to experience it directly and see it work for the children. For that to happen we need to have children with different needs and abilities, backgrounds and personalities, interests and talents together in interesting environments playing alongside each other with appropriate adult support. Nothing is more powerful than seeing inclusive play in action.

Creating a framework to support inclusive play

The *Play Inclusive Research Report* suggested that:

> We can rethink play ... by placing play at the centre of a framework for inclusion. By doing so we see that play can both influence, and be influenced by:
>
> ■ values and attitudes (ethos).
>
> ■ practice.
>
> ■ the environment.
>
> ■ the role of adults.
>
> ■ policy.

(Casey, 2004: 26)

Valuing inclusive play means taking active steps to put play at the centre of thinking. The team leader can put in place: the opportunities to develop a shared understanding of the values and principles of inclusive play; regular opportunities for consultation and development of ongoing dialogue; opportunities to review, adapt and develop the environment; a strong sense of direction and policy development.

Here are some practical areas a senior worker or team leader might want to consider to create a supportive framework for inclusive play.

Resources

■ Consider whether budgets are used and allocated in the most effective way to support inclusive play.

Join with other settings or organizations to share resources or jointly raise funds.

Establish a budget that can be used flexibly to support inclusion as the occasion or opportunity arises.

Keep up-to-date information resources (inclusion practice, guidance, web-based resources) and share these with the team.

Identify specific pieces of work or items that are fundable – for example, training, play resources, outdoor development.

Identify sources of funding (see Useful information for some suggestions).

Time

Create regular opportunities to reflect on values and what they mean to practice.

Ensure that all members of the team have time to plan and reflect on practice on a regular basis, to attend training and other development opportunities, to take part in team meetings and reviews.

Put in place timescales for new things to get going, for change to happen and for progress to be reviewed.

Manage time for change – prioritizing, monitoring and evaluation.

Keep communication flowing in all directions.

Manage time flexibly – allowing scope to try out new things in different ways, for special events, switching roles, being creative about staff deployment.

People

Ensure all staff have equitable opportunities for training and development both general and specific.

Build in regular support and supervision opportunities for all staff.

Bring people in and get them involved on a regular basis, including volunteers, sessional workers, parents, grandparents.

Develop good teamwork for inclusive play, giving all team members a shared responsibility for inclusion. Practitioners with particular responsibility or skills in relation to inclusion are full members of the team.

Empower teams to have confidence in their own judgements, knowing that they will be supported by the organization.

Be available and approachable for children to communicate with you directly and work towards children's participation being a natural part of the setting.

■ Arrange disability equality training for all members of the team including managers and committee members. Equal opportunities should be about ways of working and more than simply the contents of a forgotten, shelved document.

■ Arrange an ongoing programme of training around equality issues for all members of the team.

■ Be rigorous about equal opportunities in recruitment and selection of staff.

■ Get sussed about employing disabled people. The Sure Start Unit has produced a range of resources, including publications and free downloads, which will help settings, local authorities and their Early Years Development and Childcare Partnerships to develop successful recruitment campaigns (see Useful information).

Pool of talent

There is a good business case for employing disabled people.

If you don't, you are missing out on a huge pool of potential employees with a wide range of skills and abilities.

Disabled people are equally as capable as their non-disabled colleagues. And they often bring exceptional and complementary talents to the job.

Introducing all children to disability from an early age will help encourage their appreciation of diversity. And, especially for disabled children, disabled adults can provide valuable role models.

(DfES, 2004: 6)

Stimulating development

■ Ensure basic needs in the team are met such as the need for security, respect, trust, appreciation, opportunities to develop and to be heard.

■ Bring in people with specific expertise or experience.

■ Motivate teams – ensure that members of the team can see their contribution and that it is recognized.

■ Work towards quality standards and quality assurance schemes as a way of developing the provision and motivating teams: ('Quality in Play' (London Play) and 'The First Claim' (Play Wales) are two play-specific examples (see Usful information)).

■ Encourage open and forward-looking thinking, an investigative atmosphere and remind the team that what you are doing links in with bigger issues and questions in society.

Building bridges and partnerships

- Build strong links in the community. Seek out the other people in your area who are working in play or inclusion.

- Make contact with the umbrella organizations.

- Tap into existing networks locally or nationally – consider relevant types of network such as disabled people's organizations, parent-led or environment-focused networks.

- Make sure there is time for building relationships with parents.

- Find out how your work and interest compares to that of other professionals.

- Make links to encourage all the settings locally which children do or could attend, to share experience and work more inclusively, giving children a range of accessible options for play.

Plans and policies

- Keep policies (such as admission policies) under review to identify any discriminatory clauses and take steps to rewrite or amend them. Questions might be asked such as: Are staff aware of the policy or procedure and know how to use it? Is it accessible in language and format? Has it been carefully thought out so that it does not inadvertently discriminate against any groups? Is it clear who is responsible for doing what, when and how they do it? How will it be recorded? Does it help the delivery of a service in line with aspirations, legislation and standards?

- Ensure that statements regarding inclusion are on every significant document and integral to all job descriptions.

- Ensure that there are a range of ways and levels for children to be involved in influencing and participating in decision-making processes.

- Consider who is actively involved in running and developing the setting. Are the voices of children, colleagues and parents heard?

- Take a proactive approach to providing for the benefits of risk and challenge in play with robust statements of benefits and solidly-based risk assessments.

Notice play and celebrate it

- Make an annual award in the setting for the person who has made a significant contribution to inclusive play.

- Organize days devoted to inclusive play when you invite others to share the experience.

- Document and share good practice.

- Develop submissions for external awards.

- Highlight play in your leaflets, documents and policies.

- Put up displays in a prominent place devoted to play in your setting.

- Recognize progress – have the staff team evolved a more flexible style? Are the children getting a say? Has a disabling barrier been identified and removed?

- Say thank you.

> Clear well-thought out policies, together with procedures that put these policies into practice, are the key to good practice in risk management in play provision. Policies should state clearly the overall objectives. Procedures, including risk assessment, should state how these policies are put into practice, giving guidance but also recognizing the need for professional judgement in setting the balance between safety and other goals. Such judgements are clearly multi-disciplinary in nature. For example, while they may contain an engineering dimension, of equal or greater importance is likely to be a knowledge of child development and play itself.
>
> (The Play Safety Forum, 2002: 3)

Writing a play strategy for your setting (including children in the process)

The process of developing a play policy, in children's settings brings a new focus on play, allowing it to be better understood, planned for and developed. Although play is a distinct concept, the benefits and impact of play cut across a large number of areas including health, education, physical activity, social relationships, therapeutic practice, behaviour, emotional health and well-being. Play is often fractured and considered separately as an element of each of these rather than as a primary focus (as it would be for the children). A play strategy enables these strands and the people with an interest in them to be brought together, to consider play in a coherent fashion with play at the centre.

Benefits of developing a play strategy in children's settings include:

- bringing together people from different professional backgrounds with a common interest in play;

- allowing for the development of a common understanding of play, a shared value base and agreement on definitions of play (children's rights, Article 31, the importance of a range of play, importance of play to children with disabilities, risk);

- supporting the participation of children;

- development of a deeper understanding of play and greater specific knowledge about the play environment and culture of the setting;

- greater understanding of how the roles of different members of the community of the setting can complement each other in supporting the objectives of the play strategy;

- more children accessing more satisfying and wider-ranging play experiences;

- the removal of disabling barriers;

- inclusive practices and procedures;

- inclusive environment and design;

- less adult intervention in play and more effective support where it is required;

- sustainability;

- a plan for maintaining play opportunities and environments and reviewing them regularly.

The scope of the play strategy depends on the type and scale of the provision; however, there are a number of common principles which will underlie the development of a strategy for play, including non-discrimination and the right to play, as expressed in the UNCRC.

The process of developing a strategy is an opportunity to put ideas about participation into practice. It is an area which will attract the interest and views of children and adults who have different types and levels of involvement. The process may include:

- establishing a steering group or review group which includes children and adults;

- bringing in advice or support from external organizations (for example, a play development officer or an experienced children's consultant);

- identifying one or two people with lead responsibility (overall or in specific areas) to listen, gather views and prepare drafts;

- establishing key principles which will underlie the strategy and developing a common understanding of play (through discussion, activities such as those in Chapters 1 and 2, inputs from experienced play practitioners);

- an audit of current provision and opportunities taking into account issues around quality, environment (see Figure 3.1), adults (see Figure 6.1), usage, accessibility;

- gathering and reviewing legislation, policies, standards and strategies with a bearing on play in the particular setting, for example National Care Standards, national curricula, the DDA;

- wide consultation with all the children in the setting who wish to participate and consultation with children who are potential users but currently are excluded or uninvolved;

- consultation with adults in the setting such as janitors, classroom assistants, support staff, parents, speech therapists, physiotherapists, occupational therapists; people from other settings which the children use – nursery, after school club, breakfast club, playscheme, classroom – to promote partnerships and consistency;

- gathering together information, drawing out key themes and issues;

- identification of objectives;

- preparation of the draft strategy and consultation;

- agreement of the strategy and development of dissemination and action plans.

A time frame should be established for each stage of the process, allowing plenty of time for involving people but ensuring that there is still a sense of 'moving on'. Children (or adults) do not want to be involved in endless meetings. Preparing an agenda, chairing meetings reasonably briskly, bringing concise information and having a clear purpose for each will help. Meetings intended to develop understanding and provoke discussion can be creative, purposeful and playful to support everyone's full participation. Activities such as gathering information or consultation can be delegated to individuals or small groups in between main gatherings.

The final strategy may be structured as follows:

- Broad statement of principles (vision and rationale).

- Context of the setting (for example, geographical, community make-up, policy context).

- Results of audit of existing provision.

- Summary of consultations with children and adults.

- Analysis and identification of priorities and objectives. (Adapted from Mayor of London, 2004: 51)

The strategy might also be supplemented by:

- indications of need for action plans, codes of practice or supporting guidance in relation to specific points;

- plans to ensure the strategy is widely known among all members of the community of the setting, including the children;

- plans to ensure that the strategy is embedded in practice (for example, will the strategy be included in whole-setting review processes, self-evaluation, record-keeping, and as a standing point on agendas?).

SUMMARY

■ The management of a setting plays a crucial role is establishing the ethos, the resulting practice and in turn the overall environment for play opportunities in the setting.

■ Valuing inclusive play means taking active steps to put play at the centre of thinking. It requires a shift in attitudes and values and has to be matched by policies and practices that support it.

■ The process of developing a play policy in children's settings brings a new focus on play, allowing it to be better understood and developed in a coherent fashion with play at the centre.

■ Nothing is more powerful in changing attitudes than actually experiencing inclusive play happening.

Further reading

Council for Disabled Children (2004) *The Dignity of Risk*. London: Council for Disabled Children.

Douch P. (2002) *It Doesn't Just Happen: Inclusive Management for Inclusive Play*. London: Kidsactive.

Useful information

This section provides information on the following:

- National play organizations

- Useful organizations – play

- Useful organizations – rights and legislation

- Useful organizations – inclusion

- Useful organizations – environment

- Useful organizations – other

- Curriculum and curriculum guidance online

- Play resources

- Toys

- Suppliers of playground equipment

- Advice and sources of funding

- Volunteering.

National play organizations

The Children's Play Council (CPC)
8 Wakley Street
London EC1V 7QE
Tel: 020 7843 6016
www.ncb.org.uk/cpc
(*Managing Risk in Play: A Position
Statement, Best Play* and a number of
other useful documents are available
from the CPC)

PlayBoard
59–65 York Street
Belfast BT15 1AA
Tel: 028 9080 3380
www.playboard.org

Play Scotland
Midlothian Innovation Centre
Roslin
Midlothian EH25 9RE
Tel: 0131 440 9070
www.playscotland.org

Play Wales
Baltic House
Mount Stuart Square
Cardiff CF10 5FH
Tel: 029 2048 6050
www.playwales.org.uk
(*The First Claim: A Framework
for Quality Assessment* is
available from Play Wales)

Useful organizations – play

Action for Leisure
PO Box 9
West Molesey
Surrey KT8 1WT
Tel: 020 8783 0173
www.actionforleisure.org.uk
(Action for Leisure provides a wide range
of useful information, resource leaflets
and posters)

Kidsactive
6 Aztec Row
Berners Road
London N1 0PW
Tel: 020 7359 3073
www.kidsactive.org.uk

Children's Play Information Service
National Children's Bureau
8 Wakley Street
London EC1V 7QE
Tel: 020 7843 6303
www.ncb.org.uk/library/cpis

The International Play Association
with links
to national branches
www.ipaworld.org

Games Kids Play
www.gameskidsplay.net
(A helpful online resource listing children's
games and rhymes)

London Play
Units F6 to F7
89–93 Fonthill Road
Finsbury Park
London N4 3JH
Tel: 020 7272 2464
www.londonplay.org.uk
(*Quality in Play*, a quality
assurance scheme for out-of-
school play and childcare
provision, is available from
London Play)

National Association of Toy and
Leisure Libraries (NATLL)
68 Churchway
London NW1 1LT
Tel: 020 7387 9592
www.natll.org.uk

The National Playing Fields
Association (NPFA)
Stanley House
St Chad's Place
London WC1X 9HH
Tel: 020 7833 5360
www.npfa.co.uk

NIPPA (early years organization in
Northern Ireland)
6c Wildflower Way
Apollo Road
Belfast BT12 6TA
Tel: 028 9066 2825
www.nippa.org/

PLAYLINK
72 Albert Palace Mansion
Lurline Gardens
London SW11 4DQ
020 7720 2452
www.playlink.org.uk

Pre-School Learning Alliance
69 Kings Cross Road
London WC1X 9LL
Tel: 020 7833 0991
www.pre-school.org.uk

RoSPA (Royal Society for the
Prevention of Accients) Play Safety
The Old Village Hall
Kingston Lisle Business Centre
Wantage
Oxon OX12 9QX
Tel: 01367 820 988/9
www.rospa.org.uk

SkillsActive Playwork Unit
Castlewood House
77–91 New Oxford Street
London WC1A 1PX
Tel: 020 7632 2000
www.playwork.org.uk

Sure Start Unit
Department for Education and
Skills
Level 2
Caxton House
Tothill Street
London SW1H 9NA
Public Enquiry Unit: 0870 000 2288
www.surestart.gov.uk
(The Sure Start Unit produces a
range of very useful publications
which can also be downloaded
from their website)

4Children
City Reach
5 Greenwich View Place
London E14 9NN
Tel: 020 7512 2112
www.4children.org.uk

Useful organizations – rights and legislation

Disability Rights Commission
DRC Helpline
FREEPOST
MID 02164
Stratford upon Avon CV37 9BR
Tel: 08457 622 633
Textphone: 08457 622 644
www.drc-gb.org
(A range of excellent information and guidance related to the Disability Discrimination
Act is available in a range of formats).

Copies of legislation are available to download from the website of Her Majesty's
Stationery Office www.hmso.gov.uk or to purchase from:

The Stationary Office
Tel: 0870 600 5522
bookorders@theso.co.uk
www.clicktso.com

The *United Nations Convention on the Rights of the Child* is available from The
Stationery Office (as above) or can be downloaded from UNICEF www.unicef.org/crc

Other useful websites on rights or legislation include:

- Children's Rights Information Network   www.crin.org

- 4 Nations Child Policy Network   www.childpolicy.org.uk

- Save the Children   www.savethechildren.org.uk

Children's rights websites for children and young people include:

- Article 12   www.article12.com

- UNICEF UK's youth website   www.therightssite.org.uk/

- Children and Young People's Unit   www.cypu.gov.uk

- Children's Commissioner for Wales   www.childcom.org.uk/

- Commissioner for Children and Young   www.niccy.org/
  People for Northern Ireland

- Commissioner for Children and Young   www.cypcommissioner.org/
  People in Scotland

Useful organizations – inclusion

The following organizations offer services including training, support, helplines and information. Contact individual organizations or check their websites for more details.

Action for Blind People
14–16 Verney Road
London SE16 3DZ
National information hotline: 0800 915 4666
www.afbp.org

ADDISS
The National Attention Deficit Disorder
Information and Support Service
10 Station Road
Mill Hill
London NW7 2JU
Tel: 020 8906 9068
www.addiss.co.uk

The Alliance for Inclusive Education
Unit 2
70 South Lambeth Road
London SW8 1RL
Tel: 0207 735 5277
www.allfie.org.uk/

British Council of Disabled People
Litchurch Plaza
Litchurch Lane
Derby DE24 8AA
Tel: 01332 295551
Minicom: 01332 295581
www.bcodp.org.uk

The British Dyslexia Association
98 London Road
Reading RG1 5AU
Tel: 0118 966 2677
www.bda-dyslexia.org.uk

British Institute for Brain Injured
Children
Knowle Hall
Bridgwater
Somerset TA7 8PJ
Tel: 01278 684060
www.bibic.org.uk

British Institute of Learning
Disabilities
Campion House
Green Street
Kidderminster
Worcestershire DY10 1JL
Tel: 01562 723010
www.bild.org.uk

Centre for Studies on Inclusive
Education
New Redland
Frenchay Campus
Coldharbour Lane
Bristol BS16 1QU
Tel: 0117 328 4007
www.inclusion.org.uk

Commission for Racial Equality
St Dunstan's House
201–211 Borough High Street
London SE1 1GZ
Tel: 020 7939 0000
www.cre.gov.uk

Contact a Family
209–211 City Road
London EC1V 1JN
Tel: 020 7608 8700
Minicom: 020 7608 8702
Freephone helpline for parents
and families: 0808 808 3555
www.cafamily.org.uk

Council for Disabled Children
National Children's Bureau
8 Wakley Street
London EC1V 7QE
Tel: 020 7843 6000
www.ncb.org.uk

Disability Equality in Education
Unit GL, Leroy House
436 Essex Road
London N1 3QP
Tel: 020 7359 2855
www.diseed.org.uk

Disability, Pregnancy & Parenthood *international*
National Centre for Disabled Parents
Unit F9, 89-93 Fonthill Road
London N4 3JH
Tel: 0800 018 4730
Free-text: 0800 018 9949
www.dppi.org.uk

Down's Syndrome Association
Langdon Down Centre
2a Langdon Park
Teddington TW11 9PS
Tel: 0845 230 0372
www.downs-syndrome.org.uk

Dyspraxia Foundation
8 West Alley
Hitchin
Hertfordshire SG5 1EG
Tel: 01462 455016
Helpline: 01462 454986
www.dyspraxiafoundation.org.uk

Epilepsy Action
New Anstey House
Gate Way Drive
Yeadon
Leeds LS19 7XY
Tel: 0113 210 8800
Freephone helpline: 0808 800 5050
www.epilepsy.org.uk

Equal Opportunities Commission
Arndale Centre
Manchester M4 3EQ
Tel: 0845 601 5901
www.eoc.org.uk/

Mencap
123 Golden Lane
London EC1Y 0RT
Tel: 020 7454 0454
www.mencap.org.uk

Muscular Dystrophy Campaign
7–11 Prescott Place
London SW4 6BS
Tel: 020 7720 8055
www.muscular-dystrophy.org

The National Autistic Society
393 City Road
London EC1V 1NG
Tel: 020 7833 2299
www.nas.org.uk

The National Deaf Children's Society (NDCS)
15 Dufferin Street
London EC1Y 8UR
Tel: 020 7490 8656 (voice and text)
Freephone helpline: 0808 800 8880 (voice and text)
www.ndcs.org.uk
(NDCS provide excellent fact sheets, leaflets and other resources aimed at children, families and professionals many of which are also available to download online)

Parents for Inclusion
Unit 2
70 South Lambeth Road
London SW8 1RL
Tel: 020 7735 7735
Freephone helpline: 0800 652 3145

Royal National Institute of the Blind
105 Judd Street
London WC1H 9NE
Tel: 020 7388 1266
Helpline: 0845 766 9999
www.rnib.org.uk

Scope
PO Box 833
Milton Keynes MK12 5NY
Tel: free information service 0808 800 3333
www.scope.org.uk

Sense
11–13 Clifton Terrace
Finsbury Park
London N4 3SR
Tel: 020 7272 7774
Textphone: 020 7272 9648
www.sense.org.uk

Triangle
Unit E1
The Knoll Business Centre
Old Shoreham Road, Hove
East Sussex BN3 7GS
Tel: 01273 413141
www.triangle-services.co.uk
(Triangle is an independent organization providing training and consultancy relating to disabled children and young people. Most work is around children's rights, child protection, communication and inclusion)

YoungMinds
102–108 Clerkenwell Road
London EC1M 5SA
Tel: 020 7336 8445
www.youngminds.org.uk

Useful organizations – environment

Centre for Accessible Environments
70 South Lambeth Road
London SW8 1RL
Tel/Textphone: 020 7840 0125
www.cae.org.uk

Grounds for Learning
Airthrey Cottage
University of Stirling
Stirling FK9 4LA
Tel: 01786 445922
www.gflscotland.org.uk

Groundwork UK
1 Kennington Road
London SE1 7QP
Tel: 020 7922 1230
www.groundwork.org.uk

Learning through Landscapes
3rd Floor
Southside Offices
The Law Courts
Winchester SO23 9DL
Tel: 01962 846258
www.ltl.org.uk

National Learning Institute (NLI)
College of Design
200 Pullen Road
NC State University
Raleigh, NC 27695–7701
USA
www.naturalearning.org
(The NLI's key aim is to promote the importance of the natural environment in children's daily experience through creating stimulating environments)

ODPM (Office of the Deputy Prime Minister) Publications
PO Box 236
Wetherby
West Yorkshire LS23 7NB
Tel: 0870 1226 236
Textphone: 0870 120 7405
www.odpm.gov.uk
(*Making Play Spaces More Accessible to All: A Good Practice Guide* is available to download from the ODPM website)

Useful organizations – other

The Audit Commission
1st Floor, Millbank Tower
Millbank
London SW1P 4HQ
Tel: 020 7828 1212
Textphone: 020 7630 0421
www.audit-commission.gov.uk
(Useful information to download including fact sheets for parents of disabled children)

Health and Safety Executive (HSE)
HSE Infoline
Caerphilly Business Park
Caerphilly CF83 3GG
Tel: 08701 545 500
Minicom: 02920 808537
HSE Infoline: 08701 545 500
www.hse.gov.uk
(Very useful information is available to download free from the website)

The Child Accident Prevention Trust (CAPT)
18–20 Farringdon Lane
London EC1R 3HA
Tel: 020 7608 3828
www.capt.org.uk

Curriculum and curriculum guidance online

England

- Qualifications and Curriculum Authority
- QCA: sets of material on diversity and inclusion
- National Curriculum Online

www.qca.org.uk

www.qca.org.uk/ages3-14/6166

www.nc.uk.net

- Statutory inclusion statement on providing effective learning opportunities for all pupils — www.nc.uk.net/nc_resources/html/inclusion.shtml

- The Early Childhood Unit — www.earlychildhood.org.uk

- Sure Start — www.surestart.gov.uk

- Department for Education and Skills (DfES) — www.dfes.gov.uk

- National Curriculum in Action — www.ncaction.org.uk

- National Grid for Learning — www.ngfl.gov.uk

Wales

The Foundation Phase curriculum is planned as a progressive framework which spans over four years (3–7 years) to meet the diverse needs of all children, including those who are at an earlier stage of development and those who are more able. The pilot began in 2004.

- Qualifications Curriculum and Assessment Authority for Wales — www.accac.org.uk

- Welsh Assembly Government, Play Policy — www.wales.gov.uk/subichildren/content/play.htm

- Children in Wales — www.childreninwales.org.uk

Scotland

- Learning and Teaching Scotland (including Early Years Online and Inclusive Education) — www.ltscotland.org.uk/

- Partnership agreement from the Scottish government prioritizing play — www.scotland.gov.uk/library5/government/pfbs-04.asp

- Scottish Qualifications Authority — www.sqa.org.uk

- Children in Scotland — www.childreninscotland.org.uk

- Scottish Schools Ethos Network — www.ethosnet.co.uk

Northern Ireland

- Department of Education Northern Ireland   www.deni.gov.uk

- Pre-school guidance   www.deni.gov.uk/preschool/ preschool_curricular.pdf

- Northern Ireland Council for the Curriculum, Examinations and Assessment   www.ccea.org.uk/

- Standing Conference on Teacher Education, North and South   www.socsci.ulster.ac.uk/ education/scte/index.html

- Children's Services: Northern Ireland   www.childrensservices northernireland.com/

Play resources

Many interesting resources for play can be gathered up very easily and cheaply. The following are good sources of recycled, reclaimed, multicultural and generally interesting and unusual resources and ideas.

- Scrapstores: the following websites should help you locate local schemes:
    - www.recycle.mcmail.com/scrapsto.htm
    - www.come.to/scrapstores.uk
    - www.childrensscrapstore.co.uk/links/links.htm
- Development education centres: find a local one at www.dea.org.uk/dea/a_to_z_of_members.html
- 'One world' or 'fair trade' shops
- Also worth a browse for play resources, positive images of culture, international perspectives and children's rights are:
    - www.newint.org/shop
    - www.traidcraftshop.co.uk
    - www.oxfam.org.uk/

Resources suggested in Table 1 are intended as a starting point based on the use of natural and recycled materials and materials that can be easily gathered through requests to parents or bought cheaply. You should always use some judgement to ensure that resources are suitable before giving them to children. In particular pay attention to small loose parts, which may pose a choking hazard, or potential triggers of allergies.

Table I Resources and sources.

Play	Suggestions	Suggested sources
Dressing up Identity play	Fabric, hats, uniforms, theatrical, costumes everyday items, scarves, feather boas, fans, masks, face paints	Charity shops and jumble sales Letter sent out to parents Fabric shops Letters sent out to theatre companies, uniformed organizations (police, fire brigade, Brownies), to businesses (hard hats, boiler suits, reflective jackets)
Games	Balls, strings, chalk for markings, perhaps a parachute, books of games	Local shops for resources Ask parents and grandparents to share games they remember Bookshops and websites for ideas
Dens	Semi-permanent/outdoors: tools, wood, ropes, planks, tyres, branches etc. Temporary/indoor: fabric, blankets, cushions, table, stools	Sources: local parks or forestry department for branches, look out for work being carried out in woodlands and parks or even gardens and ask for donations Letter sent out to parents requesting donations Furnishing store Timber merchants
Sand and water	Buckets, spades, plumbing tubes and pipes, carts, guttering	DIY stores Hardware shops Builders merchants
Art	Rollers, paintbrushes, wallpaper, cardboard boxes	DIY shops Art and craft suppliers Factory off-cuts and ends of rolls Electrical stores (for large boxes)

Sensory environments	Old sheets, parachute, netting, rolls of wallpaper, curtains, willow, tissue paper, tinsel, fairy lights, fabric, cardboard, spray paint, glue, big paintbrushes, sequins, glitter, ribbons, buttons, corks, shiny fabrics and papers, dried beans, pasta, couscous	DIY shops Haberdashery shops Supermarkets Charity shops 'One world' shops Music shops Craft shops Home stores Outdoors
Wheeled play	Wheels, castors, axles, bells, reflectors Old tyres Velcro to make foot straps	DIY stores Bike shops, toy stores Tyre-fitting companies Haberdashery or craft shops
Creating small areas	Plastic garden gazebo, tent, a shower curtain, garden shed, sheets over a climbing frame	DIY and home stores Camping shops Letter to army (tents)
Toys and games from various countries and cultures	Traditional crafts, games, toys, customs and stories, everyday items such as cooking utensils, typical clothing fabrics	Borrow from toy libraries 'One world' or fair-trade shops Development education centres Hire/Borrow from local museums Ask local families from different cultures to bring in examples Internet sites Give families a small budget if they are planning a trip and ask them to buy small items to bring back
Outdoor storage	Sheds Old shipping containers Purpose-built storage	DIY stores Contact shipping companies Specialist storage firms

Toys

■ The Good Toy Guide is published annually by the National Association of Toy and Leisure Libraries. Toys are tested by both adults and children with nominations for innovation and inclusion. See NATLL details above.

- Royal National Institute of the Blind Toy Catalogue is available free by calling 0845 702 3153.

- CAPT (see details above) produces a number of safety leaflets including *How Safe Are Your Child's Toys?*

Catalogues can be obtained from the following companies offering equipment for inclusive play, including resources for sensory environments, indoor play, switches, indoor play equipment, soft play, various styles of swings and bikes and trikes. (Note: this selection and the following section of suppliers of playground equipment is intended to give a starting point only and does not confer particular merit over other sources not included.)

The Festival Shop Ltd
56 Poplar Road
Kings Heath
Birmingham B14 7AG
Tel: 0121 444 0444
www.festivalshop.co.uk

Persona Doll Training
51 Granville Road
London N12 0JH
www.persona-doll-training.org

Magic Planet
5–7 Severnside Business Park
Severn Road
Stourport-on-Severn
Worcestershire DY13 9HT
Tel: 01299 827820
www.magic-planet.biz

Rompa
Goyt Side Road
Chesterfield
Derbyshire S40 2PH
Tel: 0845 2301177
www.rompa.com

NES Arnold
Findel House
Excelsior Road
Ashby Park
Ashby de la Zouch
Leicestershire LE65 1NG
Tel: 0845 120 4525
www.nesarnold.co.uk

SpaceKraft Ltd
Titus House
29 Saltaire Road
Shipley
West Yorkshire BD18 3HH
Tel: 01274 581007
www.spacekraft.co.uk

NRS (Nottingham Rehab Supplies)
Findel House
Excelsior Road
Ashby Park
Ashby de la Zouch
Leicestershire LE65 1NG
Tel: 01530 418650
www.nrs-uk.co.uk

Suppliers of playground equipment

Catalogues of outdoor play equipment can be requested from the following companies, many of whom will also provide design services and site visits.

Hags Play
Holwell Road
Kings Stag
Sturminster Newton
Dorset DT10 2BA
Tel: 01258 817981
www.hags.co.uk

Lappset
Henson Way
Kettering
Northants NN16 8PX
Tel. 01536 412612
www.lappset.co.uk

Jupiter Play and Leisure Ltd
Unit 14
Swanston Steading
109 Swanston Road
Edinburgh EH10 7DS
Tel: 0131 445 7989
www.jupiterplay.co.uk

Sutcliffe Play Ltd
Waggon Lane
Upton
Pontefract
West Yorkshire WF9 1JS
Tel: 01977 653 200
www.sutcliffeplay.co.uk

Kompan Ltd
20 Denbigh Hall
Bletchley
Milton Keynes MK3 7QT
Tel: 01908 642466
www.kompan.com

Timberplay Ltd
Aizilewood's Mill
Nursery Street
Sheffield S3 8GG
Tel: 0845 458 9118
www.timber-play.com

Advice and sources of funding

www.governmentfunding.org.uk
This site contains valuable up-to-date information and advice about funding. It is an online portal to grants for the voluntary and community sectors from the following funders:

- Department for Education and Skills

- Department of Health

- Home Office

- Office of the Deputy Prime Minister

- Government Offices for the Regions.

www.lotterygoodcauses.org.uk
This site provides information on how to apply for Lottery funding, the latest news on the organizations that distribute Lottery money, and case studies on projects that the Lottery has funded in the past.

www.dsc.org.uk
Directory of Social Change (DSC) is a publisher of books and periodicals on fundraising and funding sources. It is a national charity providing training, research and publications. Information on grant-making trusts is available on CD-ROM and from its website www.trustfunding.org.uk

Other websites offering funding information are:

www.fundraising.co.uk
This is a free site which includes links to funders' websites, book lists, training courses and other resources linked to fundraising.

www.funderfinder.org.uk
FunderFinder is a charity that produces software for grant-seekers.

www.volresource.org.uk
This is a free source of useful information on anything to do with running a voluntary organization (whether a community group, charity, or other non-profit body).

www.green-space.org.uk/Funding/index.htm
This section of the GreenSpace website provides useful guidance notes and tips for making applications, as well as details and links to funding bodies and support organizations.

Members of Grounds for Learning and Learning through Landscapes can download funding information (see addresses above).

The Pre-school Learning Alliance has fact sheets to download from www.pre-school.org.uk/iacontent.php/en/12.phtml

Volunteering

Volunteering information around the UK can be found at the following websites:

- England   www.volunteering.org.uk
- Northern Ireland   www.volunteering-ni.org
- Wales   www.wcva.org.uk
- Scotland   www.vds.org.uk

Bibliography

Adams, S., Alexander, E. Drummond, M. and Moyles, J. (2004) *Inside the Foundation Stage: Recreating the Reception Year*. London: Association of Teachers and Lecturers.

Armitage, M. (2001) 'The Ins and Outs of the School Playground: Children's Use of "Play Places"', in Bishop, J.C. and Curtis, M. (eds) *Play Today in the Primary School Playground*. Philadelphia: Open University Press.

Ball, D.J. (2002) *Playgrounds – Risks, Benefits and Choices*. London: Health and Safety Executive.

Beels, P. (2004) 'All about Documentation', *Nursery World*, 5 February, 15–22

Bilton, H. (2002) *Outdoor Play in the Early Years: Management and Innovation*. London: David Fulton Publishers.

Blatchford, P. (1998) *Social Life in School: Pupils' Experiences of Breaktime and Recess from 7 to 16 Years*. London: Falmer.

Casey, T. (2003) *School Grounds Literature Review*. Edinburgh: Play Scotland/Grounds for Learning/sportscotland.

Casey, T. (2004) *The Play Inclusive Research Report*. Edinburgh: The Yard.

Clark, A. (2004) *Why and How we Listen to Young Children*. London: National Children's Bureau.

Cooper, V. and Blake, S. (2004) *Play, Creativity and Emotional and Social Development – Spotlight Briefing*. London: National Children's Bureau.

Council for Disabled Children (2004) *The Dignity of Risk*. London: Council for Disabled Children.

DCMS (Department for Culture, Media and Sport) (2004) *Getting Serious About Play: A Review of Children's Play*. London: DCMS.

DfEE (Department for Education and Employment) (2001) *Building Bulletin 94: Inclusive School Design*. Norwich: The Stationery Office.

DfES (Department for Education and Skills) (2004) *Recruitment and Retention of Disabled People: A Good Practice Guide for Early Years, Childcare and Playwork Providers*. London: Department for Education Skills and the Department for Work and Pensions.

Dickens, M. (2004) *Listening to Young Disabled Children*. London: National Children's Bureau.

Douch, P. (2002) *It Doesn't Just Happen: Inclusive Management for Inclusive Play*. London: Kidsactive.

Equal Opportunities Commission Scotland (undated) *An Equal Start: Promoting Equal Opportunities in the Early Years*. Glasgow: Equal Opportunities Commission Scotland.

Evans, J. (1989) *Children at Play: Life in the School Playground*. Australia: Deakin University.

Hart, R. (1997) *Children's Participation*. London: Earthscan/UNICEF.

HM Inspectorate of Education (2002) *Count Us In: Achieving Inclusion in Scottish Schools*. Edinburgh: The Stationery Office.

Hughes, B. (2001) *Evolutionary Playwork and Reflective Analytic Practice*. London: Routledge.

Humphries, S. and Rowe S. (1994) 'The biggest classroom', in Blatchford, P. and Sharp, S. (eds) *Breaktime and the School: Understanding and Changing Playground Behaviour*. London: Routledge.

John, A. and Wheway, R. (2004) *Can Play Will Play: Disabled Children and Access to Outdoor Playgrounds*. London: National Playing Fields Association.

Kidsactive (2004a) *Inclusion Checklist for Settings*. London: Kidsactive.

Kidsactive (2004b) *Inclusion Framework for Local Authorities*. London: Kidsactive.

Lancaster, Y.P. (2003) *Promoting Listening to Children: The Reader*. Berkshire: Open University Press.

Maneeterm, L., Chuntawithate, P. and Casey, T. (2001) *Play for Life*. Bangkok: Foundation for Child Development.

Marl, K. (1999) *Accessible Games Book*. London: Jessica Kingsley Publishers.

Mayor of London (2004) *Draft Guide to Preparing Play Strategies*. London: Greater London Authority, Children and Young People's Unit.

Moore, R. (1973) 'Open space learning place: school yards and other places as communal resources for environmental education, creative play and recreation', San Diego: Department of Landscape Architecture, University of California.

Murray, D. (2004) *Pick & Mix: A Selection of Inclusive Games and Activities*. London: Kidsactive.

Murray, J. (2002) *Building on Success: Case Studies of Ethos Award Winners 1997–2001*. Edinburgh: Scottish Schools Ethos Network.

NICCEA (Northern Ireland Council for the Curriculum, Examinations and Assessment) (1997) *Curricular Guidance for Pre-school Education*. Belfast: NICCEA.

NPFA (National Playing Fields Association) (2000) *Best Play: What Play Provision Should Do for Children*. London: NPFA/Children's Play Council/PLAYLINK.

ODPM (Office of the Deputy Prime Minister) (2004) *Developing Accessible Play Space: A Good Practice Guide*. London: Office of the Deputy Prime Minister.

Pettitt, B. and Laws, S. (1999) *It's Difficult To Do Dolls: Images of Disability in Children's Playthings*. London: Save the Children/Action for Leisure.

Play Safety Forum (2002) *Managing Risk in Play Provision: A Position Statement*. London: Children's Play Council.

QCA (Qualifications and Curriculum Authority) (2000) *Curriculum Guidance for the Foundation Stage*. London: QCA.

Qualifications, Curriculum and Assessment Authority for Wales (2004) *The Foundation Phase in Wales: A Draft Framework for Children's Learning*. Cardiff: ACCAC.

Reiser, R. (2003) *Everybody In. Good Practice in the Identification and Inclusion of Disabled Children and Those with SEN: A Guide for Practitioners and Teachers*. London: Disability Equality in Education.

Rennie, S. (2003) 'Making play work: the fundamental role of play in the development of social relationships', in Brown, F. (ed.) *Playwork: Theory and Practice*. Buckingham: Open University Press.

Scottish Consultative Council on the Curriculum (1999a) *A Curriculum Framework for Children 3–5*. Edinburgh: Scottish Office.

Scottish Consultative Council on the Curriculum (1999b) *A Curriculum Framework for Children 5–14*. Edinburgh: Scottish Office.

Scottish Executive (2001) *Better Behaviour, Better Learning: Summary Report of the Discipline Task Group*. Edinburgh: the Stationery Office.

Scottish Executive (2002) *Guidance on Preparing Accessibility Strategies*. Edinburgh: The Stationery Office.

Shephard, C. and Treseder, P. (2002) *Participation: Spice It Up!* Cardiff: Save the Children Fund.

Society for Children and Youth of British Columbia (undated) *Making Space for Children, Rethinking and Re-creating Children's Play Environments*. Vancouver: Society for Children and Youth of British Columbia.

Stirling Council Children's Services (undated) *Inside Out and Outside In*. Stirling: Stirling Council.

Sutton-Smith, B. (2001) *The Ambiguity of Play*. Cambridge, MA: Harvard University Press.

Titman, W. (1994) *Special Places, Special People: The Hidden Curriculum of School Grounds*. Godalming: World Wide Fund for Nature/Learning through Landscapes.

UNICEF (1989) Convention on the Rights of the Child. Online: www.unicef.org/crc

Widdowson, J.D.A. (2001) 'Rhythm, repetition and rhetoric: learning language in the school playground', in Bishop J.C. and Curtis, M. (eds) *Play Today in the Primary School Playground*. Philadelphia: Open University Press.

Index

acceptance, atmosphere of: 38–39
accessibility of inclusive environment: 40
activities and exercises: 22–23
adults
    facilitating role: 56–57
    planning role: 86–90
    risk and challenge, role in: 68
    supporting role: 86, 87, *Fig. 6.1*
art
    ephemeral: 83
    outdoor: 81–84
assessment of environment *see* auditing
        inclusive environments
attitudes to inclusive provision, changing:
        99–100
auditing inclusive environments: 43–51, *Fig. 3.1*
award for inclusive play: 103

barriers to inclusive play: 12–13
benefits of inclusive play
    for children: 18–19
    for children's settings: 19–20, 30
    generally: 18–30, *Fig. 2.1*
    for society: 20
'Best Play' objectives: 15, *Fig. 1.1*

case studies
    communication, facilitating: 65–66
    environment, improving: 31–32
    environment, influence of: 34
    modelling inclusive behaviour: 67
    objectives of inclusive play: 16
    risk and challenge: 41, 68
    scaffolding of play: 62–63
centres of interest, in inclusive environment:
        37
challenges in inclusive play: 13–14
celebration of play: 103–104

children
    additional support needs, with: 3
    benefits of inclusive play for: 18–19
    consultation of: 24–30
    disabilities, with: 3
    disabled: 3
    participation of: 24, 25, *Fig. 2.2*, 51–53
    use of term: 3
Children Act 1989: 10
'children with disabilities'
    use of term: 3
    value of inclusive play for: 20–22
communication
    in consultation with children: 27
    within play, facilitating: 64–66
community of setting
    benefits of inclusive play for: 20, 30
consultation of children: 24–30
continuity of indoor and outdoor environments:
        42–43
creative input
    generally: 69–70
    identity, play with: 73–75
    sensory environments: 70–72
    wheeled play: 75–76
curricula
    inclusive play and: 14–15
    online guidance on: 115–117

DDA *see* Disability Discrimination Act 1995
dens and hideaways: 79–81
designing inclusive play environments: 52–54,
        Fig. 3.2
development plan, for play environment: 53,
        Fig. 3.2
disability, medical and social models of: 10–11
Disability Discrimination Act 1995 (DDA): 10
Disability Rights Commission (DRC): 10

'disabled children', use of term: 3
discussion starters, on inclusion: 7
documentation of play: 90–93, *Fig. 6.2*
DRC *see* Disability Rights Commission

environments, inclusive play
   acceptance, atmosphere of, in: 38
   accessibility in: 40
   art objects integrated with: 83–84
   assessing *see* auditing *below*
   auditing: 43–51, *Fig. 3.1*
   centres of interest in: 37
   continuity of indoor and outdoor: 42–43
   designing: 52–54, *Fig. 3.2*
   development plan for: 53, *Fig. 3.2*
   flexibility in: 36
   influence on inclusive play: 32–33
   natural features in: 38
   organizations for, information on: 114–115
   participation of children, improvement
      through: 51–53
   place, feeling of, in: 38–39
   qualities of: 34–43
   risk and challenge in: 40–41
   sensory elements in: 39
   shelter in: 36–37
   workshop on: 51
ephemeral art: 83
ethos of setting: 97–99

facilitating inclusive play
   adults, role of: 56–57
   communication: 64–66
   fears, overcoming: 57–60, *Fig. 4.1*
fears, overcoming, in development of inclusive
     play: 57–60, *Fig. 4.1*
flexibility, in inclusive environment: 36
framework for inclusive play, creating
   celebration of play: 103–104
   development, stimulating: 102
   introduction: 100
   partnerships, building: 103
   people: 101–102
   plans and policies: 103
   resources: 100–101
   time: 101
funding, information on: 121–122

games, use of: 77–79

identity, play with: 73–75
inclusion
   definition of: 4–7

discussion starters: 7
   integration and: 11
   organizations for, information on: 112–114
inclusive behaviour
   habits of: 98
   modelling: 66–67
inclusive play
   activities and exercises: 22–23
   attitudes to, changing: 99–100
   barriers to: 12–13
   benefits of: 18–20
   case for: 9–11
   challenges in: 13–14
   creative input in: 69–85
   and curricula: 14–16
   definition of: 4–7
   dens and hideaways: 79–81
   documentation of: 90–93
   in early years: 4–17
   environments for: 31–55
   facilitating: 56–68
   factors influencing: 12–14, 32–33
   framework for, creating: 100–104
   games, use of: 77–79
   identity, play with: 73–75
   intervention in: 61
   involving people: 93–96
   managing for: 97–107
   observation of: 90–93
   opportunities for: 12, 56–68
   outdoor art: 81–84
   participation culture supporting: 24, 25, *Fig.
     2.2*
   planning for: 86–90
   sensory environments: 70–72
   strategy for, developing: 104–106
   supporting, adults' role in: 86, 87, *Fig. 6.1*
   value of: 18–30
   wheeled play: 75–76
integration and inclusion: 11
intervention in inclusive play: 61
involving people: 93–96

legislation, organizations on: 111
'low intervention, high response': 61

managing for inclusive play: 97–107
memories of play: 8
modelling inclusive behaviour: 66–67

national play organizations, information on:
     108–109
natural features, in inclusive environment: 38

observation of play: 90–93
observation sheet, sample: 91, 92, *Fig. 6.2*
opportunities for inclusive play
　enabling: 56–68
　generally: 12
organizations, information on
　environment: 114–115
　generally: 115
　inclusion: 112–114
　play: 108–110
　rights and legislation: 111
outdoor art: 81–84

'parents', use of term: 3
participation, children's
　culture supporting inclusive play: 24, 25,
　　Fig. 2.2
　improving play environment through: 51–53,
　　Fig. 3.2
place, sense of: 33, 38–39
planning for inclusive play: 86–90
play
　celebration of: 103–104
　identity, with: 73–75
　inclusive *see* inclusive play
　memories of: 8
　organizations for, information on: 108–110
　resources for *see* resources for play
　scaffolding of: 61–63
　strategy for *see* play strategy
　wheeled: 75–76
play strategy, writing: 104–106
playground equipment, suppliers of: 121

resources for play
　dens and hideaways: 80
　in framework for inclusion: 100–101
　games: 78
　identity, play with: 74
　information on: 117–119, **Table 1**
　outdoor art: 82

transforming environment: 71–72
　wheeled play: 76
risk and challenge, in inclusive environment
　adult's role in supporting: 68
　importance of: 40–41
rights, organizations for promotion of: 111

scaffolding of play: 61–63
SENDA *see* Special Educational Needs and
　　Disability Act 2001
sensory elements, in inclusive environment:
　　39, 70–72
settings, children's
　benefits of inclusive play for: 19–20, 30
　communities of: 20
　ethos of: 97–99
shelter, in inclusive environment: 36–37
Special Educational Needs and Disability Act
　　2001 (SENDA): 10
strategy *see* play strategy
supporting inclusive play, adults' role in: 86, 87,
　　Fig. 6.1

'teams', definition of: 3
terminology: 3, 4
toys, information on: 119–120

UNCRC *see* United Nations Convention on the
　　Rights of the Child
United Nations Convention on the Rights of
　　the Child (UNCRC)
　and consultation of children: 24
　contents of: 9

value of inclusive play
　for children with disabilities: 20–22
　generally: 18–30
volunteering, information on: 122

wheeled play: 75–76
workshop, on play environment: 51